From the Roots to the Fruits:

Becoming a Tree of Righteousness

Teresa Pearsall-Young

ISBN: 978-1-955312-48-6
Printed in the United States of America
Story Corner Publishing & Consulting, Inc.
1510 Atlanta Ave.
Portsmouth, VA 23704

Storycornerpublishing@yahoo.com
www.StoryCornerPublishing.com

Dedication

To Mommy, **Ludie Mae Pearsall**, wishing you were here, but it comforts me to know you are at peace. You taught me so much!

To Daddy, **Albert James Miller**, I know you would be proud. Loving you both always and forever!

To my sisters, **Linda Carol Bond** & **Gwendolyn Faye Colburn**, I still think about dialing your numbers to tell you what's going on, and must remember that I can't, but I can still talk to you both as you are still in my mind and my heart. Things are well sisters. Rest.

To my dearly departed cousin in love, **Carl Patterson**, you were a great addition to the family, even if only for a short time. I wish you were here to see the dream that you supported finally manifested. As an author you were a great writer and I learned by reviewing and helping you with your manuscripts. You never stopped pushing me to get my book done. I must give you your props. It's finally happening.

To all the special lives we have lost through these last few years to due COVID 19, or due to seen and unforeseen illnesses, I loved and miss each and everyone of you. *Brother Curtis Miller, Aunt Christine Barron, Bahiyahdeen Ali (Uncle Bobby), Arthur Miller (Uncle Mikey), Cousin Juanita Miller, Gloria Cooper, Cousin Stewart Barfield*, I thank God for the memories that will never be replaced.

TABLE OF CONTENTS

Acknowledgements

For those of you who thought it not robbery to purchase my first book **'Seeds, Trees. Branches & Leaves,** I thank you and I am truly grateful and humbled. This book was and still is my baby. It has opened doors for me. If you don't have it yet, you need to get it for your library.

I want to thank you for purchasing my second book, **'From the Roots to the Fruits, Becoming A Tree of Righteousness'.** The journey continues.

I must first thank my heartbeats, my daughter **Syreeta L. Pearsall**, through the struggle you have never lost hope. **Your Life Matters!** I love you to life. The audible is coming.

To my grands, **Tejsia Gladden, Aramayya and Tasneem Upshur**, you keep me laughing and on my toes. I love you all.

To my son-in-love, **Jehmar Gladden**, I have prayed for the day, after 24 years, to be able to say, 'Welcome Home!' Thank you, Lord, you are free.

To my husband, **Pastor Anthony Young**, well, you're keeping me Young. Thank you for your ministry, your prayers, and your constant support and your love.

To my cover artist and niece, **Steddy Chanjin**, once again, you have captured exactly what I have asked for, every time. We're a team. Thank you! I love you.

To my leaders, Apostle Timothy & Pastor Michelle Brinson you have been and remain a powerful impact on my life. Thank you for all you have taught me on the kingdom of God and for keeping me as your spiritual daughter. You are my family.

Dr Leonard Robinson, thank you for your tireless teaching on the kingdom of God, the more I learn the more want to know.

To my sister **Erica Parker Jordan**, thank you for always instructing on Turning your Pain into Power. As we continue to give testimony and write about overcoming our struggles and finding joy in living the kingdom life, we are only getting stronger every day. I love you.

To my niece, **Grenita Hall**, thank you for the push to get my first book done; your words matter. You are and have been a true inspiration, a seeker of the kingdom, and a 'doer' of God's word. Keep on writing! I love and appreciate you.

To **Story Corner Publishing & Consulting, Inc.,** once again, you are making my dream come true. Your vision has helped many see their vision come to pass. Thank you for your sacrifice and your obedience.

Chapter 1

From The Roots

From the Roots- Intro

Root: the under growth from the bottom part of a plant body, grown from a seed, that functions as an organ of absorption, aeration, and food storage or as a means of anchorage and support,

Other 'root' definitions: pertaining to hair (new growth), the end of a nerve, the part of an organ or object that is attached to another body part or object (the root of the tongue). Dentists may need to perform a 'root canal' on your teeth

(The **love of money** is the root of all evil) **1 Tim 6:10** (KJV)

Root Cause: "The main cause for or why a problem keeps occurring,"

The basic reason (or reasons) that can be identified, that a person has the power to fix.

Rooted & Grounded': The word says Jesus is Love. I understand this to be true because I believe in Him. Believers are taught to be 'rooted and grounded' in the word and our Lord and savior, Jesus Christ. The word teaches of His love, and Jesus is the root (foundation) of how we are to live. Being rooted and grounded in love means to be rooted and grounded in Jesus Christ.

Jeremiah 17:7-8 7 Blessed is the man that trusteth in the LORD, and whose hope the LORD is. 8 For he shall be as a tree planted by the waters, and that spreadeth out her roots by the river, and shall not see when heat cometh, but her leaf shall be green; and shall not be careful in the year of drought, neither shall cease from yielding fruit. (Bible Gateway – KJV)

Colossians 2:6-7 6 As ye have therefore received Christ Jesus the Lord, so walk ye in him: 7 Rooted and built up in him, and stablished in the faith, as ye have been taught, abounding therein with thanksgiving (Bible Gateway – KJV)

Ephesians 3:16-19 16 That he would grant you, according to the riches of his glory, to be strengthened with might by his Spirit in the inner man; 17 That Christ may dwell in your hearts by faith; that ye, being rooted and grounded in love, 18 May be able to comprehend with all saints what is the breadth, and length, and depth, and height; 19 And to know the love of Christ, which passeth knowledge, that ye might be filled with all the fulness of God. (Bible Gateway – KJV)

Matthew 13:6 6 And when the sun was up, they were scorched; and because they had no root, they withered away.

It is important for us to understand our 'roots'. Many people research family trees to determine the history of previous relatives that they may or may not have known. Results allow them to discover genealogical history of relatives or conditions in their families. This may uncover reasons they do a certain thing or act a certain way, or it may reveal secrets or abuses they may not have been aware of, i.e. - 'Root Cause'.

Before being made well or made whole, like the woman with an issue of blood, it is helpful to discuss or write about issues or situations that may have been the 'root cause' of some past bitterness, pain, abuse, relational or generational situations. Expressing these issues, in any form can be a help to letting go of the heavy on your brain so that you can heal and be healed the way God wants you to. God's purpose for your life was not to remain wounded. In the first book, Seeds, Trees, Branches & Leaves, I shared with you a glimpse of how God changed my life, through the good, the bad and the ugly. In this book, **From the Roots to the Fruits: Becoming a Tree of Righteousness**, the journey continues.

I have included poems, stories and stoetrys that describe issues that were the root of different situations. Some of the writings are personal and some regarding personal situations that were not my own, but valid.

The expression was needed to help myself or others to deal with hurt and pain from the 'bitter roots' of the situation and determining the 'root cause.' Being rooted and grounded in love means to be rooted and grounded in Jesus Christ. However, there is a process to getting there. The goal is to receive healing and learn to demonstrate the love of Jesus Christ. Let the journey continue.

Ain't Nobody Ask You

So, this morning, I was in a funk, feeling a plethora of emotions
Staring in the mirror, thinking I was going to have a talk with myself,
knowing that I should be further along in life
That no one could see through my masquerade, that I was struggling to live right for Christ
Staring at myself, trying to delve into my soul
There has been as many setbacks as there has been breakthroughs, but why?
As I stared at my soul, what I thought was my subconscious mind, turned out to be the voice of the Lord.

'My dear, it's time to confess to yourself, to your mess
You're trying your best to live by my word, but is it your best?
You want me, you need me, but you're still a captive longing to be free
So many times, I've been there for you
Yet you give me 50% and I'm blue,
You must get off the see saw, I am on the high end and you're still sitting low.
Catering to the gleam in your eye, the weakness in your mind
Being satisfied for a few quick moments, then thirsting for me after
Promising me ultimatums, if I get you out of the jam, once again
You want everything that I have for you, thus sayeth the Lord
But you must let go completely, of the 'unclean thing'
'Well Lord what do you mean the unclean thing?'
He said 'my dear, an unclean thing is anything that is unequally yoked with me.

Addictions, lusts, gluttony, clutter, lifestyles that honor Satan, not me

My dear, you have struggled to change your life, and you have changed,

but that bounce back anointing keeps bouncing in the wrong direction, and this is by your own election

My dear, you crawl, you walk, you cry, you hurt, you find me, you get renewed, you regain your strength, you come alive again, you get healed in the heart and in the mind

You praise me, you get better for a minute

But then your mind wanders back to the mess, it's as if your soul is possessed

You can't survive a reprobate mind, but Jesus will take you back every time.

You must become convinced of me

So, you will stop returning to the enemy

Dig deep within yourself to get to the root cause, discover the origin to put your pain on pause.

You are a woman of resilience, I see your hurt, and your fear that someone will uncover your dirt

You are dependent on being depended upon, it's in plain view

Focus on why the Lord needs you. Fix yourself and stop trying to fix others

As you pray that your issues are not discovered.

Confession, admission, however you choose its only dead weight that you're choosing to lose.

Be truthful with yourself, admit what you did wrong, so it does not happen again.

If you would not have gone to that party, if you wouldn't have met that man, if you wouldn't have been searching for fun, you may have been a little further in me

Stop looking for someone to blame for your shame, Prepare a place in your heart for me and my name

Come clean and come to me.

#Ain'tNobodyAskedYou!

Graphically Speaking,
Get Rid of The Coat

A coat has been hanging,
In my closet,
Full of memories.
Negative, filthy, nightmarish memories
Reminders of corner waiting, devastating, visually
graphic memories
A coat, reminding me of a world I no longer see
As I claim to be set free, graphic memories calling me

Well, my soul says to me 'answer, if you dare!'
Why is that coat still there?
if that world Is said and done
And your kingdom walk has begun
You have changed your definition of fun
Wasn't it the street life that made you run?

Run? For the border? No, run to Jesus!
Only he could re-conceive me
He was sent to redeem us
Well, my soul says to me, you need to bury the past
Allowing your new garment to last
No need to hold on to what is wrong and should be
gone

You don't need the reminders
Of the wounds that have begun to heal
By toiling in the field
Of redemption and salvation
Don't break the consecration
The gospel highway is my new location
Now.
Remove the coat and bury the past
Set the shame on fire, its overdue to expire
The coat, too small, too large, it no longer fits

In my coat of starting over, I had to repent
I am renewed in discovering
There's no peace, no warmth in that old covering
There is only one divine being that's hovering
That is Jesus and the kingdom
It's the new life for me, Jehovah Nissi
I'll take the king size comforter

My name is CAPTIVE: I am a Pain-acholic

Skeletons in my closet, bad memories in my head
I'm a captive, weighted down and living life in hell, instead
Holding on to too much baggage, I can't get no quick relief
If I'm crying you a river, how do I turn pain to peace?
Do you hear me? as I share with you, the hurt inside of me
Yes, Hello! My name is CAPTIVE, praying God will set me Free

Hiding early childhood troubles, being sworn to secrecy
I wish I knew God's power then, He would have rescued me
Growing older, overweight & bright but pretty, nonetheless
Always someone's hidden treasure, never treated like the rest
Life was rough and times were tough,
With bleeding heart. Most times I cried
Well, Hello! my name was BROKEN, but God taught me to survive

Young in childbirth, learned a lesson, but became a single parent
Not yet saved, but doing better, still not being that transparent
In came drugs, abuse so hurtful and oppression came my way
Friends were killed with no prediction, as addictions came to stay
Lost some family, nephews vanished, are they dead, are they alive?
My Granddaughter's father jailed, conspiracy to homicide

My health was not my wealth, my strengthened faith helped me to pray
Hello! My name was VICTIM, but He took the pain away

I was stressed, life was a mess, I surely made some desperate moves
The crazy loves I'd found just left me feeling drained and sorely bruised
My husband gave me many gifts but barely was I glad
Reminded me of childhood days, he drank, just like my dad
The Curse, not cure, destroyed him with his daughter's suicide
4 months to follow, tragedy, with her sister's homicide
His hidden grief allowed no peace, a broken man, he cried!
HELLO, my name was HEARTACHE, and this pain I could not hide

Looking long for perfect love, found, but cloned, in all wrong places
Guarding tender heart and self from so called friends that have two faces
No acceptance, just rejection, needing God to Rescue Me
Crowded me, not proud of me, Lord, change my mind to clutter free
Pray, Speak, forgive, wipe the clutter from my mind,
Letting Go and Letting God, help me sweep the pain behind
Now dependent on His Power, no longer food for Satan's devour.
This is my story of the hour
My name is OVERCOMER, Turning Pain into Power

Needed

Adam was busy for Eden
But there were no living things like him
God knew what Adam **needed**
So, from God's great idea,
He gifted Adam a helper
Already existing, then created.

Made, also in His image & likeness
Immaculately brought to life
A Female Being.
Needed before she was wanted
With God's hand, she became.

A necessary ingredient for humanity,
Uniquely designed by God above
Made for Adam and given in love

God's divine creation,
The first operation on earth.
Needed,
to birth Kings & Queens, generations,
All races & whole nations

The woman was a word before she was.
God said 'I will pull a woman out of this man'
As Adam slept, his dream was coming true
Flesh of his flesh, bone of his bone.
Man could not live by bread alone.
What Adam **needed** was inside of him. The woman was
an inside job
God was inside of them both

Created, not from dust, but from Adams rib,
Birthed, Not conceived,
In a garden of trees

Fully grown & compatible
Born, unlike an infant,
Adam's helper was God's needed intent!

From God's breath, He gave her life
With breasts, warm to caress,
Lips soft to kiss, supplying portals for intimacy and seas of reproduction,
For creation of a world that **needed** constructing.

Formed as a woman, not a weapon
Made not as man, but from man,
God gave her a 'womb with a view'
With the ability to multiply and subdue
Historically a miracle, but God came through

A woman, body by God
Created as man's helper suitable,
A soul that was beautiful
Woman, female, she, her,
She was called & chosen, and created a stir
From the beginning......

With her creation, man became 'male & female'
Them equaled him & her
Going forward they created boys and girls
Adam named his woman Eve,
The mother of all living
Needed, first as a wife, then as a mother and queen of giving Her **purpose**,
to help Adam and be God's helping hand,
A **needed** seed for mankind to breed, Birthing all populations, indeed.

Already given dominion,
A first of millions, within one

Even after the serpent whispered her to shame
That woman did what was needed to recover her name
Without her the world would not have been the same

Before her creation, she existed & was completed because
God was aware of what Adam
Needed!

Noah & the 'F' Principles

Noah's grandfather was Methuselah. At the age of 187, he sired a son, Lamech. Methuselah had other children at age 782. He lived to be 969 years old. That is where the saying comes from, old as Methuselah. The kids must have finally worn him out.

At the age of 182, Lamech sired a son and named him Noah. Noah means comfort, rest, or relief. Lamech had other sons and daughters at age 595. He lived to be 777 years old. The kids must have finally worn him down. Noah was 500 yrs old when he had Shem, Japheth, and Ham, in that order. (Better known as The Migos, BC)

The Flood

The earth began to populate with men and women of all types and characters. The Lord said, **"My spirit will not contend with man forever. Man is mortal and his days will be a hundred and twenty.'**

God put a limit on the madness. He decided that 120 years was long enough to put up with man on this earth. You will note in the Bible it took a while for the mortality rate to drop, but at the beginning of mankind men at that time lived for centuries. (Today, if someone makes it to 50, they're doing good!)

The Lord had created man on this earth, but He saw that man was evil and wicked all the time, and it upset Him. He decided to wipe mankind from the face of the earth, as well as creatures of the ground and birds in the air.

But Noah found **favor** in the eyes of the Lord.

Noah was a righteous man, and the bible says God would not see the righteous **forsaken. God did not forsake him.** Noah was **fearful** of the Lord. He walked with God.

After God saw how corrupt the people of the earth had become. He told Noah 'I am going to put an end to all people, because the earth is filled with violence because of them. I am surely going to destroy both them and the earth.' God was **fed up**. *(What do you think God is thinking about the world today?)*

Noah's profession was a shipbuilder, and a **farmer**. He also had a love for animals, and God knew this.

God gave Noah *exact instructions* to build the ark, and Noah was obedient.

He told Noah to make an ark of cypress wood, make rooms in it, like a house, and coat it with pitch inside and out. (Pitch is a substance that's tar like)

God instructed the ark to be 450 feet long, 75 feet wide and 45 feet high. *(In Hebrew versions say it was 300 cubit long, 50 cubits wide and 30 cubits high)*

A **cubit** is the length from elbow to fingertips.

God told Noah to make a roof and finish it and make lower, middle, and upper decks.

He told Noah to take his **family**, his sons, their children, and seven pairs of every kind of clean animal, and 2 of every kind of unclean animal; 1 male, 1 female and get them on the ark.

He also told him to take all the food you need for your family and the animals.

(What type of food could they have had? After a while, it seems they would start looking at each other.)

Noah followed God's instructions. Noah was obedient. If God gave you some instructions, could you follow them to the tee? We know this is particularly hard for men, let alone, mankind. The ark was as tall as a five to six story building. God was about to wreak havoc in the joint. He was about to destroy the earth. But Noah found favor with God. God told Noah he would establish

His covenant with him.

Understand this, Noah was not a refugee, but he was an evacuee, and a chosen one at that.

If President Bush and the government and politicians of New Orleans needed to know what to do to prepare for hurricane Katrina, they should have checked Genesis: Chapters 3 – 6.

They labeled Katrina a category 5, but this great **flood** that God was preparing Noah for could not be classified. What category would you call 'earth destroying?' *'This flood is labeled 'The Wrath of God' and it's a category 9,999.'*

How many of the people in New Orleans would have loved to be in Noah's shoes or on 'Noah's ark'? God was pissed off, and when God is pissed off, you may not escape the wrath, but you don't hang around to see what He's going to do.

God knew He was going to destroy the earth, but he gave Noah time to build this ark, and time to load the animals, his family, and supplies. It took 120 years to build the ark, and about three weeks after the flood hit the earth on February 17th of that year. If the politicians of New Orleans would have checked the bible, in Genesis, they would have had an idea of how much time was needed to evacuate the city, having previous knowledge that Katrina was coming.

God said it would rain for 40 days and 40 nights and **flood** the earth.

(In today's times Forty Nights sounds like a name of a malt liquor.

Advertisement: Forty Nights, the scrapple of bottled beer.

Speaking of malt liquor, our people need to be delivered from drinking this stuff. It is liquid crack in a 40-ounce bottle. I speak from experience, and no, I don't drink it. I call it the scrapple of bottled beer because scrapple is made up of scraps of pork or other meat products. You don't know what may be in it. That is the same way malt liquor is made, anything and everything is in it. That's why folks who drink it get stupid, sound stupid and look stupid with the quickness. The warning is in the name.

Forty Nights; in one night, you'll feel like you've been drinking for 40 days and 40 nights.

Steel Reserve: it's like drinking melted down scrap metal.

St Ides: remember 'beware the Ides of March', Julius Caesar was warned to 'beware the Ides of March and killed by someone he thought was a friend on the Ides of march. Some folks think St. Ides is their friend. Et tu, saints & sinners? You better beware St. Ides in the hood.

Old English, what can I say, it's furniture polish, would you drink furniture polish?

Colt 45, it's a loaded gun, or a bullet in a bottle.

Hurricane – we all know that a hurricane is a natural disaster, and when that hurricane works itself up in you, you're in the bathroom like it's a natural disaster. People please be delivered.

Let's get back to Noah. God told Noah to 'Go into the ark, with your family because I have found you righteous in this generation'. **Are you righteous in your generation, righteous enough to be chosen for the kingdom?**

Currently Noah was 600 years old. On (February 17th) the floodgates of heaven were open. Noah's **family**, and animals, and creatures got on the ark, all except the fish, they lived in the water, so it was no need for them on the ark. Then God shut the chosen in to protect them from the devastation of the flood.

The rain came and the floods rose and destroyed the earth and destroyed every living thing that moved, man and creatures. **The chosen were afloat on the ark**.

It rained for 40 days and 40 nights, but the earth remained flooded and finally receded after 150 days. That was a five-month period. People only hear about the 40 days and 40 nights, but Noah and his crew were on the ark much longer than that. We think Katrina was bad, imagine water 20 feet high in your city, or your town for 5 months.

But then God remembered that Noah was out there on the water, floating. It was a **smooth** transition to the ark. It was **great** to be chosen and not be destroyed, with the rest of the mankind. Noah and his family were **floating** on the water that covered the earth. **Smooth, Great, Float**. With God remembering Noah, he sent a wind over the earth to dry up the water and the waters receded.

On the seventeenth day of the 7 month (July 17th,) the ark came to rest on the mountains of Ararat, in Turkey.

The waters continued to recede by the 10th month on the first day (October 1) and finally the mountaintops were visible.

Going back, being afloat for so long, Noah opened a window on the ark and sent out a raven. Imagine after almost 5 months of people and animals living in a shut-in environment, like the Katrina victims in the New Orleans superdome, it was time to open a window. Thank God for **fresh** air. The raven was glad to get out. The raven kept flying back and forth within those 150 days because it was looking for dry land. Then Noah sent out a dove to see if the dove would return to the ark. The second time the dove was sent, it returned with a twig from an olive tree. The next time the dove was sent, it didn't come back. I wonder why. The dove found a place to land and build its nest, and it didn't want to go back to the stench.   The dove was the **first evacuee** to find a new home after the destruction created by the flood.

I'm sure the people and the animals on the ark rejoiced, first to be alive and spared, and then to get the hell off the ark.

Noah was 601 yrs old when he removed the covering of the ark to see that the earth was completely dry. By February 27th of the following year, the earth was completely dry.

God told Noah to come out of the ark with his family and animals, so they can multiply on the earth, and be **fruitful** and increase mankind. Here was God once again trying to establish what he had already started with Adam and Eve. In Genesis 1- 28, after he created man and woman, he blessed them and said be fruitful, multiply, replenish and subdue, then take dominion. With Noah and his descendants, God was giving mankind a second chance and the same rules applied this time.

So, they came out of the ark and Noah built an altar to the Lord. He sacrificed burnt offerings on it from some of the clean birds.

God then said that never again would He curse the earth because of man, even though every inclination of his heart is evil from childhood. God was stating that we are born in sin, from our first minute on earth. From an infant, we need to be working on our heart to live for the good, not the evil. (*This is why some parents start beating the 'hell' out of their children from day one.*)

God said, never again will I destroy living creatures as I have done. The keywords here are 'as I have done'. So, he did not plan on destroying any living thing in the same magnitude as he had destroyed the earth with this flood, but later in time we would see that He was going to do what he had to do. His wrath has been shown at different times, in different areas of the world, and in different capacities like the tsunami, the mudslides, the earthquakes and the hurricanes. God is not playing with us, folks we better get it right.

God said, 'As long as the earth endures, seedtime and harvest, cold and heat, summer and winter, then day and night will never cease.' But the earth must endure. Are you sure you can endure?

God blessed Noah and his sons, who are descendants and ancestors of all of us. *That's right, he was Uncle Noah.* God granted that all would fear Noah and his family including creatures, and that food would be supplied by everything that lives and moves. God gave Noah status. Upgrade with lemonade, he had it made in the shade.

God said, 'Just as I gave you the green plants, I give you everything!

Could you imagine what it would be like to hear from God himself the words 'I give you everything'? That would be big-time Favor. *I would head straight to the Escapade dealer and then to that 3-million-dollar house that I saw in the magazine. Well, He said everything!*

God established covenant with them and said never again will there be a flood to destroy the earth, or will all life be cut off from the earth. The sign of the covenant was the rainbow in the clouds. The covenant was set for generations to come. Whenever you see the rainbow after the rain, remember that represents our covenant with God.

Noah had three sons, Shem, Japheth and Ham. From them came the people that were scattered over the earth. Now, the earth is big, and all I can say is there had to be a whole lot of baby-making going on to start a whole earth. This is not family, a community, city, or country, we're talking about earth. *And if the earth was restored by the descendants of Noah, quiet as it's kept, there was incest going on, because they were all related. So, people were jacked up from way back when. Back then there was no Viagra, and the men and women lived to be centuries old and were centuries old before they even had children. Some of you are thinking 'if you could only turn back the hands of time. Be delivered.*

Noah was a **farmer** as well as a shipbuilder and he planted a vineyard. Noah drank some of the wine from his own vineyard, and he became drunk. He had too much of his own product. *Has anybody ever had too much of their own product? Ask the folks to raise their hand. Very few will raise their hands so tell them they're lying.* This is one story that attracted me to learn more about Noah. There are people near and dear to my heart who tended to drink too much of the wrong thing. And they claimed to love God, well who am I to judge. But if Noah was a righteous man, what would possess him to drink too much wine. This goes to show that when you are highly favored, the enemy will do whatever he can to expose something negative about you. Even the most righteous man could fall short before the glory of God. Therefore, we must always keep God with us, always. *If you're going to the bar, take God with you. Sit Him right on the stool next to you. By the time you finish talking to God on that bar stool, someone will be looking to escort you out, on the pretense that you've had too much. At that time God will surely be working on your behalf.*

When Noah got drunk, he passed out. Sound familiar?

('Noah, what's wrong with you?' "I'm just tired, that's all.")

This is something he would have never done if he had been in his right mind. He was consumed by the spirit of the juice. This wasn't even Jesus juice. Why would Noah want to get drunk? First, he had already lived to be 601 years old. If being alive on earth for over 600 years isn't enough to be drunk about, what is? Then, he had just been taken through a horrendous storm that totally wiped out the entire earth. He had also endured being on an ark with his family. Could you endure being with your whole family in the same house for almost five months while floating on water and you can't even go outside or open a window? Hell no! Not only was his family on the ark but also a bunch of wild, stinking animals, bugs, and elephants. Could you imagine shacking up with some big old elephants and their poop? I would just like to know which deck were they on, the bottom, middle or the top? Noah and his family had also been given the responsibility of populating the earth. Noah was stressed out and had probably been sipping his own product for a while.

Noah passed out in his drunkenness and was naked and exposed. Here is a righteous man exposed in his sins, drunkenness, and nakedness. His youngest son Hamm found him drunk and naked, and he went to tell his brothers how he found his dad.

His two sons Shem and Japheth, came to cover Noah with a blanket, when they reached him, they walked in backwards and covered him before they turned around, so they would not see his nakedness.

When Noah awoke and was told of what happened, he was very angry with Hamm (not himself) for his discovery. He was so upset that he decided to curse Hamm's son Canaan, and he bade him to be the lowest slave to his brothers and the slave of Shem and Japheth. With the favor God had given Noah, you would have thought that he would have found **forgiveness** in his heart for his son Hamm. After all Hamm did not get Noah drunk and strip him, Noah did this to himself.

Noah was hurt that he had been exposed. Think about the word exposed, and then think about the word posed in exposed.

To pose is to voluntarily model or stand to show others.

If one poses for a picture they are saying yes, take my picture, and capture my move. You don't mind people knowing about these moves. These are the pictures you show. However, when you're **exposed**, you've been uncovered, your secret has been told, the picture was taken without your permission, someone has put you on front street. Thanks to the enemy, your business is out.

Everything was cool because no one knew about Noah's drinking. He tried to be so discreet. Remember, discreet is the enemy. There is a secret in the word discreet. If it's undercover, it's not for you, God lover.

Noah, a righteous man was exposed. But the flip side is this, since he didn't admit his problem, if he had not been exposed, he may have continued his stinking drinking, and he may not have been cured of his problem. *Could you see Noah at an AA meeting saying, 'Hi, my name is Noah, and I'm an alcoholic'.*

In Noah's exposure, he was hurt and needed someone to blame for his embarrassment. I would have thought that he may have had a talk with Hamm, tried to explain to him, apologize for being found this way, and let him know that he need not share this with anyone else, and then seek help. But instead, he cursed Canaan, the son of Hamm, an innocent person in the whole situation, but Noah cursed him to be a slave, not his son Hamm who exposed him or himself who drank too much wine from the vineyard. My conclusion here is even a righteous man can fall short. You need to take control of the things that may be controlling you and handle your own exposure. You are still righteous in His eyes, so never let go of God. To expose the enemy at any cost is the goal, **free** yourself, and then there will be nothing for you to be bound by. Tell your own dirt, and then tell your testimony as to how God moved on your behalf.

Even for Noah, God continued to move, he lived another 349 years, until the age of 950 and then he died.

The 'F' Principles

Favor– Noah had **favor** with God. Learn to recognize God's favor in your life.

Fearful– Noah was **fearful** of God. Learn to be God loving and God fearing.

Fed up– God was **fed up** with mankind. Make sure He's not **fed up** with you.

Family– Noah was blessed, therefore so was his **family**. Your **family** may be blessed because of your salvation.

Forsaken– As a righteous man, Noah was not **forsaken** by God.

To be righteous or to be **forsaken**? That is the question.

Flood– Noah and his family and the animals were protected from the **flood**. Don't wait for the **flood** to come before trying to get to a higher place.

Forgiven– If Noah was favored by God, Hamm should have been **forgiven.** Learn to forgive and pray to be forgiven for your mistakes.

Fruitful– After the flood, Noah and his descendants were instructed to be **fruitful**. Be **fruitful**, multiply, replenish and subdue as in Genesis 1 -28.

Found– Noah was **found** drunk and naked in his sleep. Don't wait to be **found** out by someone else, free yourself.

Fresh– The **fresh** air was appreciated after being shut in on the ark for so long. After living in unbearable conditions, it is great to be able to make a **fresh** start.

Farmer– A **farmer** sows a seed and expects a harvest. If we sow like the **farmer**, we reap what we sow. The harvest should be many times greater.

Free– Take off your mask, **free** your mind of what binds you up and let your soul be **free**.

From Pain to Joy

A song of pain is in your heart, in your head
You've been hurt by what was done to you or said
You want to kill the pain, shoot it dead
So, you go get a gun and figure
If you aim at the temple and pull the trigger
That pain can't hurt you anymore

Pain will no longer set its feet inside your door
Although, it had once dropped you to the floor
That could have been the way it would be
But just in time, you realize to die is not the remedy
The drain and strain of the pain is messing up your life
So, you search for a knife to make it right

Because you want to cut it out, while you scream and
shout
But it's the doubt that stops you
It's not the right thing but it's so frightening
Question, what becomes of the broken hearted?
The unspoken hearted, with hope now departed.
Bad memories from painful roots that started it.

The blinds that were always closed
So, the abuse is not exposed
So, nobody knows your pain
And you think one day the hurt will go away
But it's just lying dormant in the format of unknown
Because the truth is not full blown
Didn't you know that pain is a color of the enemy
He uses it to fill the inside of you and me
The outline is a shell of emotion
It is not just a notion that pain stems from abuse
To women and men, thou can be loosed
To let it go! You dare not show what's true
You hold it in and stay undercover blue

The problem reoccurs again and again
Letting pain win. To maintain pain is a sin.
Pain and abuse go hand in hand
This emotion does not discriminate between woman or man
Hurt people hurt other people
The depth of pain is so deep
The flooding of pain will drown you

As you wear your pain like a crown heavy on your head
After being hurt by what one did or said
Don't surrender, don't give in
You can be rescued and begin again
You must train yourself to regain
Your life and your power from your pain
You can stand up and reclaim your name
Hurt and abuse has no gain
As you help yourself flee from the enemy
You can set another captive free, it just might be me
Be a little bolder; train yourself to be a shoulder
For those who are still hurting that are even a little older
You have lived with the abuse and the shame
You can reclaim your life in Jesus's name
You'll be surprised by far when God shows you who you really
He'll remove the mask and fear and allow you to persevere
Folks will stand up and cheer
To know you've been rescued from pain so severe

The painful memories have not disappeared
But no longer control your actions
Your lifestyle is changed and will impact someone
When they see you about town with your head up, no frown
As you smile and give someone a pound

When you expose the enemy at any cost
Get busy! cleaning out your closet
You know your heart has become a project
With a lot of issues packed inside
Because you keep taking them along for the ride
As you spring clean your brain
Did you know that dirt and pain are one and the same?
Hiding in the cracks and crevices
Get busy sweeping the pain out of your life
And begin to live
Get into every crack and corner of your mind
You know that cracks kill!
When you have done the housekeeping of your brain
You have reduced pain to a mere smack of the enemy
Instead of an attack of the enemy
There is no more hush hush
Tell someone even if you tell yourself
Remember being discreet is a trick of the enemy
It is self-induced abuse; there is a secret in discreet
Expose the enemy at any cost
Laugh in the enemy's face, show your joy!

Thank God for being a survivor!
Thank Him For faith and perseverance
And the ability to progress in spite of the mess
You will no longer cry because of pain and what you
have endured
Your song of pain will not be sang
Your mindset will show you're on the road to sane
As you are now in control and your pain has turned to
joy
Joy is now your gain

Set Me Free -Lord, Please De-Wife Me

There are meeting rooms, for people with all types of problems. There is a room for AA Alcoholics Anonymous, and NA for Narcotics Anonymous, there's even a room for family members of Alcoholic and Narcotics Anonymous, but there is no meeting room for WA – Wifey Anonymous.

Well, what do you mean Teresa? Well, I'm glad you asked.

You see the bible says in **Proverbs 18 v22** -He who finds a wife finds a good thing and obtains favor from the LORD.

But when he finds a wife, does he find the good thing that then becomes his wife, or does he find a former wife, someone that's living as single that still operates in 'wifey mode'.

So, I am a member of the Wifey Anonymous club, there is no such thing but I'm thinking about starting one. I say that because I am not married, as a matter of fact, I was married, then I divorced my husband and then reconnected with him, and then separated from him again. Not too long after, I became a widow. To me, he was always my husband, and I was with him until his last breath. But I moved straight from caring for and then mourning him, to wife mode with another man. No, I didn't get married again, that time, but my mindset was still in 'wifey' mode, to help and take care of a man,

Even though, at that point, I should have been operating in 'Single – Good thing' Mode. Some feel I should have still been in mourning, but they had no clue about the relationship between me and my ex-husband. You see, I had given him my all, and it was too much. He gave me his all; all of his issues, all of his problems, all of his sicknesses, so I was carrying his all and mines. We got divorced, he moved out, and we stayed separately for about 2 years until my insecurities brought him back to the home, thinking something was better than nothing, it wasn't.

I had spoken before about acting out of desperation, yet there I was again, acting out of desperation.

The relationship between me and my ex was worse than the first time. After a year he moved out again. But he was horribly sick. He had told me he had gotten better, and was going to counseling, he had stopped drinking. All lies. But I be wanted to believe them, and I think he did too. But I was the dummy!

So, not too long after he moved out, he was placed in hospice care, and he decided then to fight for his life. He was in hospice for almost two years before he lost the fight.

You see, before he passed, I was already tired and frustrated. I was mad at myself because I was free, we were divorced, but I still cared. I didn't know how to care about him from a distance. So even though we were divorced, I was still looking after him in wife mode. I believed every lie that he told me, that he was seeking psychiatric help, he had cut down on drinking and smoking, he was going to the doctor regularly.

I was afraid to jump in something with someone else. I was used to him. Once his foot was back in the door, it was worse than what it was the first time. After a year, he was out again. Not to long after, he was in the nursing home, and that's where he would live for the next two years and his final days.

My ex-husband was my friend and I stuck with him until the end. There was history between us from years before we ever married. It was the good, the bad, and the ugly. We divorced, and he is now deceased, but I stuck by him until his last breath, because for him, no other person could do anything like me, and he was the only husband I ever had.

I continued to go see him, help him, take him shopping when needed. And he still cared for me and his grandchildren. He told me he wished he had treated me better. It was just too late.

I also started dating someone else during that time, *looking for love in all the wrong places.* After all I Was divorced, even though I was still caring for my ex-husband. I wanted to finally have some fun. My past years had been rough, I was hoping to find life again.

The man I was seeing had issues as well, but a little more kept. Truth was he had major issues that I didn't recognize immediately, because of the smoke screen of feeling finally rescued for life. He was a narcissist, and I didn't know. A true career military man. At first, I was impressed, as was everyone that met him, but before long, I was turned off.

I did not know how to get out of it, so I stayed, for a while. The lifestyle I was living with him was not becoming to me, I was the front, the trophy to show while they styled and profiled. But really, he didn't have it going on. He was military madness at its best. What I realized, is that I had not given myself time to be de-programmed from being a wife. My body was single, but my mind still operated in wife mode.

What happens when you are in between relationships? If you have never been a wife, or lived in that capacity, then you can function as a single woman. There are single ministries, and there are marriage ministries, but where is the ministry for the in-betweeners.

In my mind and heart, I am still operating in wife mode, and I can't help it! I have been many things including single, married, divorced, and widowed, in a relationship and back to single, but I cannot get the wifey out of me.

You see, I have learned through experience that, we, well let me speak for myself, I truthfully, I don't know how to stop being a wife.

I figured it out, it's because I was in wife mode for so long, that I don't know how to turn off the wifey button. I believe that I am not the only female that faces this problem.

Ladies, as soon as we meet a man, we prefer to see God in the man, but if there is potential in the 'prospect', we size them up, and start thinking about how we can clean them up, make them better, or convince them to live for Christ, while learning to perform their husbandly duties, before they are even our husbands.

When we see a 'prospect', we start selling our wifely skills. Telling them how good we can cook. And then we start to feed them, thinking that we're paying it forward.

As a single woman, we should be expecting to be invited out to dinner or let him offer to cook a meal.

The next thing we do, is offer to share the cost, such a wifely thing to do.

Married couples share the cost. Remember, as singles, we need to let him pay. If your worth it to him, he will pay. If you don't practice this, before you know it, you'll be paying the whole bill.

The next thing we do, is start picking up after the man, trying to straighten up his place, and him.

So, there we go showing him how we can cook and clean and put his life in order.

There we go trying to control him, when he calls and when he's supposed to come by, and then you're worrying about who else he's calling and seeing, if he doesn't come by.

I know that I am that person, and I am learning to enjoy doing things as a single, but I'm still in wifey mode. I need rehab.

You see my wake-up call occurred recently. I had a

friend whom I liked, but who had traits and issues that annoyed me. We were starting to do many things together, but when certain things started getting on my nerves, I started to complain about him.

I complained to a friend one day, and her words have stuck with me ever since.

She said, 'Teresa I heard your cry, and I get your point, but I'm afraid to tell you, sweetie, you don't have the right to tell him what to do with his money, or his time, or his health cause you ain't nobodies' wife! You ain't his wife. And He ain't your husband.

It might be convenient to him that y'all are playing husband and wife over here, then husband and wife over there, but if that man dropped dead today or tomorrow, what would you have?

A back seat is what you would have, cause you ain't nobodies' wife. His family would step in and there wouldn't be anything you would have except an opinion. No truer words were ever spoken, and they have stuck with me ever since.

So, there are 2 minutes you need to watch out for when you are in wifey mode, but not the wife.

The minute that you have gone too far with your wifey control, and it's no longer what he wants to see or hear from you, or if he really has someone else in mind, dude is going to be quick to remind you, 'You are not my wife!'

The other minute is the minute that you have an expense or need help with something that he's been partaking in all this time and enjoying, but now you need help, a large bill or repair in the house, he is going to remind you that, I am not your husband, I don't know who you going to call to help with THAT, but it won't be me, cause you ain't my wife, and that ain't my house!

Now here is my truth.

I don't want to be single. And I am truly in love with God as many of us are. I do want a friend or companion, but in preparation for marriage. Note to self: If you are still preparing for marriage after a few years with the same man, it's time to check the situation.

But I am also a firm believer that your Boaz will find and pursue you, and you should not be searching for him because you want a man. You don't want to make a wrong decision from a desperate vision. You might find out later that you are stuck with someone that it is not so easy to live with or get away from.

You would be the blame because you couldn't wait. WAIT is such a strong word.

It is not better to have someone than no one at all if it is not the right person.

Remember how we used to say as kids, if you like it so much, why don't you marry it? If you want to be a wife, be a wife to yourself, get your own self in order.

Cook for yourself, clean for yourself, and take yourself out, better yet, take yourself to church, or fellowship, impress yourself on how smart you are, and make your own self pray. Save yourself!

 (In the words of Shakespeare, 'to thine own self be true')

Save your own money. Fellowship with others that are single like you, you'll be surprised at who you might find and that it can be fun having single fellowships with other people, not just two.

I also feel awkward around all married couples, because I feel like the little kid who shouldn't be in the room when grown folks are talking married stuff. I have been there, done that, got the t-shirt and the hat. But just not now.

I'm confessing that I need to be de-programmed, I need to be

de-wifed, so that I can be single enough for my Boaz to find me and be His good thing for real.

God doesn't grant unauthorized authority in somebodies' life, just because you're acting like somebody's wife.

You can quickly be let down by unrealistic expectations.

The other issue many of us have is that our 'help you' sign shines a little too brightly, so it flows from the men in your life to family and friends. It should be a good thing to help people sometimes, but we must learn to use wisdom in helping. This is hard but sometimes you must learn to play dumb and play it well. When folks share with you and ask for your advice, just learn to say 3 little words, I DON'T KNOW! Learn how to stop trying to fix other people's problems, when you have a basket full of problems yourself. My name is Teresa, and I am a former wife. I am now single, and I don't know diddly!

In August of 2021, I remarried. We were equally yoked and have known each other as friends for over 11 years before we ever considered having a relationship with each other in this capacity. We both loved God and are determined to keep God in the relationship in every way. Sometimes your Boaz is right under your nose, and you never realize it. It's been one day at a time, with God and prayer.

Sleep Apnea

In a dream
everything was fine
sheep were counting me
until something cut off my breath
I realized I could not breathe
through my mouth or my nose
I could not move
I was immobilized!

In my ear I heard God say
'Get up! Move! Breathe! '
Suddenly, I came out of the coma
Choking and gasping for air
Trying to take a breath
I began to thank the Lord
'Thank you, Lord!
Thank you, Jesus!
Thank you, Father!'

I was frightened
I realized a minute longer I might have died
But God would not let me go out like that
He woke me up!
Now if that is not a reason to praise him then what is?

So grateful that
In my sleep an angel was watching over me
The angel recognized my dilemma
The angel said 'Breathe! Wake up! Breathe!'
But I did not hear it, immediately.
I was immobilized!

So, God willed it. His will be done
Then I heard Him
So, I breathe, I choke, I gasp

and I wake up!
Halleluiah!

The angel was the stand in
This was God's assignment to him
Thank the Lord!
Thank you, Jesus!
Thank you, Father!
if this is not a reason to praise him
Then what is?
Hallelujah!

Sleeping With the Enemy

We can blame the enemy for many things
For everything that has gone wrong or keeps going
wrong
But if you look in the mirror
Don't be surprised when you come face to face with
your true enemy.
You'll see you, Your inner me.
The enemy lies within because we struggle
Against evils not always recognizable.
The goal in life is to walk a righteous path, but detours
and roadblocks make the struggle real
I got in my own way!
Knowing there should be no compromise but letting the
enemy or the inner me take over.
Constantly being taken advantage of, because the inner
me cannot say NO!
Just say no to drugs, to abuse, to any excuse, just say
Noooo!
Being strong in the day, strength is needed at night, for
the dreams and thoughts of the enemy that seem nice
but are not right.

So, this morning I woke up, alone
I looked around and in rising,
I recognized no one was home
Still holding the dream of who I thought I could be
What was holding me back I realized was me.
I was my own worst enemy

Not my own best friend.
I was the person with a climb that never ends
Lord, you gave me visions of who and what I should be
But goals were impossible to reach if the enemy was me
Even in growth I keep holding me back
It's time to tell self-doubt to stop the attack

I have a giving heart, working hands, and can't say no,
but now is the time to let God, and Let go
Running from excuse to abuse, by God's grace it's time
for me to be loosed
I'm ready to break the pattern and chains from
committing the same crimes, living my own sentence
while doing enemy time
God said, 'You can, and you will, it's time to shine!'
The Lord gave your yours and he gave me mines
So much for His glory, telling His and my story
Sharing lessons learned, fires burnt, desires yearned
Carrying hurt over my head, but I put it in a basket and
set it down instead
I found the inner me can be the enemy if you don't
learn to set yourself free
I thank God for deliverance, no more nightmares or
frightmares for me
I can now sleep peacefully and wake up with who God
made me to be.

Take Off the Mask

Come out, come out wherever you are
You are a child of God to be blessed by far
Accepting the Lord can be quite a task
To free yourself please take off the mask

In the presence of souls with composure so trained
You've become an expert in hiding your pain
You function as if you have no story to tell
But beyond the mask, in your sorrow you dwell

When will you let it all go, I ask?
Isn't it time that you take off the mask?
You say that your goal is to do ministry
Until there's a purging, you cannot be free

Look to your left and look to your right
There are people like you who have lived the same life
Your goal is new life, let the old drama end
But without inner healing, new life can't begin

When you take off the mask, you'll feel freer inside
You 'll be freed from the demons of living a lie
Your life can go forward because of your purge
Watch yourself as your talents will now emerge

No surprise that others are hiding, like you
There are many that need to unmask themselves, too
Share your story with someone whose suffered the
same
Look forward to healing unmasking will gain

Write a letter or poem or novel or two
Whatever it takes to remove the taboo
Your outside must be the reflection of in
How can you smile freely? God wants you to win.

Deliverance comes when its off your chest
This burden is lifted, and you know the rest
You can laugh, you can pray, you can say what you feel
Please take off the mask and help someone else heal.

The Spirit of Offense

The spirit of offense is a tool the enemy uses to turn
people against one another
We must learn to recognize this spirit and counter it
with wisdom
First, it takes two or more people for one to be offended
One person cannot offend oneself, unless they are
schizophrenic

It can happen with the twinkling of an eye
The spirit of offense can be powerful in a negative way.
It can turn best friends into enemies, family against
each other,
become the reason for divorce or marriage by mistake
become the reason someone runs, thinks too much or
drinks too much
become the reason for death, homicide, or suicide
becomes the reason someone leaves the church, or
doesn't come at all

All because someone was offended!
Offense can mend fences for the wrong reason
You don't want to see your relatives offended, even if
you don't like them.
Offense can put you on the defense, and can make a
situation intense
Offense will not make you smile and does not help to
reconcile
Offense can openly defile you or make you act like a
child.
Think about It, most offenders are easily offended, they
dish it out, but they can't take it.
Many people don't think before they speak, from their
mouths offensive words will leak
Some people talk down to others and we don't
understand how to receive these people, so, we are

offended!
As children of the Lord our mindset should be to 'brush it off,'
walk away, and be the better or bigger person but instead,
we take it personal

Some folks waste valuable time being offended for other people
He's mad, she's mad, so I'm mad too. Why?
We spend too much time worrying about little things
'Why does she look at me like that?' 'He never speaks to me?'
'Why wasn't I chosen?' 'I should have been the first choice!'
'They will regret this decision!' 'Are they talking about me?'
'Are they laughing at me?' 'Why wasn't I invited?'
'I thought I was their friend too!' 'What do you mean, I look nice, today!'

It behooves us to be the better person, but the spirit of offense will stop that every time.
Here is a prime example of sudden offense:
I was walking down the street singing 'The spirit of the Lord is near; the spirit of the Lord is near!' Walking down the street towards me was a sister of the nightlife.
She was a crackaloo or crackasian and she was looking pretty piped out!
When we approached each other, she said 'Hey, sister you looking kinda chunky!
The enemy had got his foot in the door just that fast!
Of course, I looked at my big beautiful, blessed self but instead of seeing the God inside I saw the picture she painted of me

I assumed that by no means did she have what I had in Christ.
The Christ in me should have said 'Yes, I am full of the Lord Jesus Christ'
I am constantly fed in his word.' However, my offended spirit thought
'I'm looking kind of chunky but you looking kind of funky!'
My reply was defensive because I was caught off guard, and **I was offended**

I replied to the crackhead, 'oh I've been away on vacation and
we did enjoy the food. I didn't think it showed that much.'
Well, the crackhead said, 'Yes it shows honey, it shows, you gotta couple dollars?'
So, what did I do, I reached in my pocket and gave her a quarter.
She took it but **she looked offended**.

I took my offended self home, I looked in the mirror, I moved my bulges from side to side.
I berated myself because of the offense
I should have been praying for the crackhead.
I should have asked her would she like to come to church with me one day
it could have been another soul saved. Instead, I let the enemy win
The spirit of offense will have you sitting and licking your wounds,
traveling roads, you normally wouldn't go down, just to avoid known offenders, taking jobs you don't want just because you said you 'Wouldn't go back to 'that' place!'

The spirit of offense will also bring out the spirit of selfishness,

stupidity and low self-esteem and one of the worst
sins, pride.
We as mature adults should learn the system of 'let it
roll.'
People will always try to step on our toes or bust that
bubble
because they will always want to question our
relationship with God.
Why do you think they tell you 'You ain't all that!'
The enemy wants to put doubt in your mind about the
power of God.

We must learn to say, 'I've been delivered, what about
you?' or 'You could have hurt my feelings if I let you,'
how about 'You be blessed anyhow!'
Don't let the spirit of offense walk and talk you out
of your blessings, your relationships, your spouse,
your business partners, your job, your birthright, your
inheritance, your man or woman of God, your salvation,
or the Kingdom of Christ.
Let nothing hinder you while reaching for the sky
Be blessed and remember,
Don't be Offended!

The Wound is Still Too Deep

I thought it I was over it
The hurt, the pain, the situation
The backstabbing
Cut, from those even in front of me,
Who were smiling.

I thought I could smile about it
I thought I could be that bigger person
I thought I would see the light about it
I thought I could sweep it under the rug,
But the lump could not be flattened
I thought that resolution was near
But whenever I opened my mouth to give a cheer

The only thing I could taste was a tear
That travelled from my heart to my eyes
I could not shake the fear, so I cried
At the idea of being hurt this way again
This cut needed more than a band aid
The debt of the wound was not repaid
The dream I prayed for was that I could now sleep,
Peacefully, and that my mind could be free
But unfortunately, negative thoughts were on repeat
Cause the wound is still too deep.

There Are No Words in Frankford

The Tale of Two Souls– Beauty & Lovely Rose

Beauty Weeps

When we received the news, it was a strange, but a sad delivery.

I walked into my home and saw my husband, at the time, in his big burgundy leather chair, where he always was, crying. There was a visitor in the room.

I asked, 'What's going on, y'all?'

The visitor said, **'He just found out that His baby girl was dead.'**

All I could say was 'Huh! Not Beauty!' What do ya mean??? Shock with confusion was written all over my face.

Beauty's favorite question was 'What do ya mean?' So, I asked "What do ya mean?'!

My face didn't believe it, and neither did my mind. This couldn't be true.

As far as we knew, Beauty was in a recovery house, being treated for substances that she was abusing and that were abusing her. She was getting better!

The last time we saw her was at her older sister Splendid's funeral. Another young life gone tragically & far too soon. First Splendid & now Beauty, barely 4 months apart. This did not compute.

The messengers, or bearers of the bad news, wanted to offer their condolences. It was one of her 'best' girlfriends & the young lady's husband, she was *Oh Mee* & and he was *Oh Mai*.

The couple had firsthand news of Beauty's death. Interesting! How did they know, so quickly?

This couldn't be. It wasn't right, it wasn't fair. We were looking forward to spending time when she came home. When you recognize the beauty of the person, apart from the addictions, that's who you look forward to spending time with, but now that wasn't going to happen.

Beauty was far too young to die. She had a heart that was finding its way to the surface.

Yet the evidence spoke for itself. The family was in shock. My husband looked as if someone had kicked him in the gut. There were few times when I have seen him cry and this was one of them.

For me, it was as much of a shock, as if she were my own daughter. You see, she was my stepdaughter, but I called her my kept daughter.

It hurt because we had truly, finally bonded. I wasn't her birth mom, who was deceased, but I was the only mom she had. Our relationship started out strained, but it grew. I never knew our last hug was our last hug.

The story was on the news, 'Breaking news....'Young black female found dead in, in a house in Frankford'. We saw the story on the news. Yes, Beauty made the news. Beauty was found deceased in that Frankford home. As sad as we thought the story was, we had no clue it was our daughter.

The rumor was that she was there to entertain a few 'gentlemen'. She always thought she was beautiful. Beauty was beautiful on the outside. But there was much healing needed on the inside, but she was starting to breakthrough, looking forward to a better life, so I thought.

This was a nightmare that you thought was a dream that you couldn't wake up from.

I'll never forget the experience of her father & I going

to the morgue to identify her body.

They wouldn't let us see the physical body, but they showed us the picture of her laying there, looking only sleep, (she loved her sleep), with the needle sticking out of her neck of where they tried to revive her. Unreal, Unbelievable, Unfortunate.

The coroner reported that the substances that were found in her system were oxycodone & crack cocaine.

Well, I knew enough about Beauty to know, that she probably knew she was ingesting the crack cocaine, but she did not know she was ingesting oxycodone. You see the crack is an up high, and oxycodone is a down high. So those gentlemen that she was entertaining had plans for her that she was not aware. All she wanted from them was for them to tell her she was beautiful. After all her name was Beauty.

The story is, when they saw her take her last breath, they jetted, left her where she lay......

The *bearers of the bad news, Oh Mee & Oh Mai,* apparently had some acquaintance with those gentlemen, else how would they know so much, so soon. These are things that make you go 'hmmm!'

Beauty could not be revived so that was the end of her beautiful life.

As troubled as she was, Beauty had a way of touching the hearts of those she met.

People did care about her, but not everyone, including the slick pimp, Nova Fox, who recovered her from the recovery house. It seems he helped her to get there, only to clean her up for what he needed to use her for, his monetary gain. Her life meant nothing to him. He gave her what she wanted to receive, told her what she wanted to hear, then used and abused her, made her think he really cared, then retrieved her to continue to use and abuse her. This is what pimps do.

All she had to leave behind, besides her family was the 'what ifs'....

What if she lived? *What if* she fully recovered?

What if she would have become the singer she wanted to be.

What if she could have made it to the age of 30. She was only 28 years young.

What If she would have had children.

We will never know.

As a stepmother, she gave me a hard way to go. I understood it and put up with as much as I could, until I couldn't put up with it anymore, but I had not given up on her.

We bonded and grew into a relationship. I understood some things even her dad did not. There were many drama-filled days. She was always willing to fight for my birth daughter, and her children. She was funny, and did things that were wrong when done, but later when we talked about it, it was funny.

All that remains are her memories.

The streets don't love our children, not in any city. She will never be hurt by anyone, ever again, including the streets of Frankford, the badlands, on the wild side of the city.

Lovely Rose

We received the call on New Year's Night 20XX. Our good friend, Paris Rose, was informed that her daughter, **Lovely**, was found in the streets of Frankford, and could not be revived. Lovely was her name. Lovely Rose to be exact.

When that news was delivered to me and my new husband, my heart skipped a beat, a pain came in my stomach, and all I could think of was my stepdaughter, Beauty, who suffered a similar death, seven years ago. At that time, I was married to her dad, who went home to be with the Lord, in 2016. It hurt then and this was the same pain. I felt it for my friend, Paris. The streets of Frankford have yet claimed another undeserving soul.

Lovely was with child, it would have been a boy. The death angel struck twice in one life.

Unfair, Undeserving, Unfortunate.

Is it really like this in this world? Are people so uncaring. Is it really dog eat dog out there? Some areas of the city really look like and feel like HELL.

My heart ached for Ms. Paris. She knew that *Lovely* loved her children that she left behind.

Ms. Paris only wanted for her daughter to get better, to be free of the demons that took hold of her.

She would have given the world for her daughter to still be here. She would have gladly dealt with raising her unborn grandson, if it meant that Lovely was still alive.

There are no words.

There is nothing anyone can say to make Ms. Paris or any mother who has lost a child to the streets feel any better.

We are not supposed to bury our children.

We want to live long to enjoy our children, then their children, and then our great grandchildren if possible.

When the streets take the lives of our Lovely Roses' and our Beauty's', we are robbed, and so is the world.

When the streets take the lives of our sons, we are robbed and so is the world.

There are no words when death occurs in the streets of Frankford, it feels like a devilish wind robbing our mothers of their children again and again and again.

Thank God that He will not allow the enemy to hurt them anymore, we would rather see Him holding our Lovely's and our Beauty's' in His arms, than to let the streets do them anymore harm. They are His, not the streets. There are no words in the streets of Frankford.

To Beauty & Lovely Rose you are now at peace resting in His arms.

Rest in Peace my babies.

Too Sweet

I remember when I was a growing young girl and
grandma would sleep in the chair
We thought she was tired from working all day, we
should have been saying our prayers
One day she had asked me to give her some milk, I
thought it would be quite a treat
I laced it with sugar but wished that I wouldn't have,
she frowned and said oh it's too sweet
I wish I'd have known her disease was full blown, they
said that my grandma had sugar
She always was tired before she expired, that's what
the disease would do to her
in 1967 grandma went to heaven and after her death
there were others
Not enough conversation about the situation, from her
blood was the way they discovered
A curse, generational, kept secret, relational, it robbed
us of Grandma's sweet hugs
I may have been saved from the life I now see using
needles with insulin drugs
Nightmares and no sleep, and a constant release of
bodily fluids in me.
No rest, did I mention, thirst was unquenchable, needed
testing for A-1C
Hungry and tired and vision now blurred. Diabetes, a
negative seed!
Though I lost so much weight the next meal could not
wait, generational curse indeed
So fatigued and stressed out with anxiety bouts, I felt
like I wanted to snap
Under much duress as I dealt with the mess, diabetes
had dealt me a slap

I left for vacation as I anticipated reuniting with family,
my stress was evident, illness not heaven sent, this was

not where my life should

in June '98, North Carolina the place, that is where the diagnosis was named

Forget the prognosis I'd never have chosen this, my life is so changed, not the same

Thank God I prayed and this world I stayed I asked God please do not take me yet

Had I known this before I would have been sure to read up on symptoms at best

Comatose for three days what a hospital stay, in Wayne County! God heard my plea

For my life, I thank God I now work on his squad I have been resurrected, you see.

Days in Ward ICU, I did not have a clue as to what had just happened to me

But my relatives did, as their worry not hidden, they watched a revival proceed

10 minutes from death, God's miracle at best, from the doctor's own mouth, it was said

it was some crazy test, but God answers requests, he revived me from being brain dead

I had to learn quickly to prick and to stick me and put on the shelf all the sweets

What I never knew was what sweetness could do, the **root cause** of my bodies defeat

God allowed me to live and to tell what He did, I could never forget this story

I learned to walk again, and as I talked again, I began to give Him the glory

Blind as blind could be, a small time not to see, this disease not a walk in the park

Too sweet by and by but I do testify, thanks to God I am not in the dark

Sugar low, Sugar high, educate yourself. Why? Learn whatever it is that you can

Don't be slow but be smart, protect body and heart,
and receive what's intended for man
Please watch what you eat, not too many sweets, the
less carbohydrates the better
Read the labels on cans and pray on demand, with your
primary care in the picture
To make the long story longer controlling my hunger,
was harder than ever before
With a new lease on life, now I am somebody's wife and
I've learned to love God even more.

Wanted- Parents 'Like Back in The Day'

Train up a child in the way he should go [teaching him to seek God's wisdom and will for his abilities and talents] Even, when he is old, he will not depart from it. **Proverbs 22:6**

Today, our children's futures are at risk
Our children don't understand it, but the levels of devils have increased,
In truth, we are all born in sin and shaped in inequity
Parents who knew the word, knew this. But back in the day, parents ruled!
Old school parents took the reins to transform the youth from birth and in infancy
*It was **preventative maintenance**, an attempt to protect our children from this wicked world.*
Teaching of violence & drugs were taboo; kids weren't allowed to get tattoos!
Teaching manners is not so much, anymore.
We laugh and think it's cute when kids act grown or rude.
***Back in the day** parents did not spare the rod, they may have spoiled the child.*
Old school parents believed in spanking, if needed, and kids were grounded for a little while
***Back in the day** there were no timeouts.*
There were lessons learned, rewards were earned.
But today, the cell phone is taken, for a minute. A soft punishment.
***Back in the day**, children learned to respect what the elders had to say.*
Unfortunately, our children no longer fear God or man.
They have become challenging and quick to demand
Our babies now idolize YouTube jockeys that teach disrespect according to world standards,
Loving grossness & stupidity; and taught subliminally, to accept the negative.

Our children of today practice manipulation, they are quick to generate empathy, when wrong,
Because, of course, they are still babies and it's not always their fault!
Many parents today, have put up the 'do not disturb' sign, forcing children to teach themselves
Many children today cuss like sailors as they have been cussed out numerous times by their parents.
A negative seed that's been sown is, 'You ain't never gone be nothing'! Some have been told.
Back in the day, teachers were great and loved to serve our kids, but today,
They are wearing the weight of many hats, becoming more hopeless than hopeful.
Parents trying to be their child's BFF, when its parenting time you cannot be that friend!
Our children today are more concerned with acceptance rather than God's presence
Certain things were never in God's plan, especially concerning the children
But the world has cleverly changed the child's mind, training wrong to be right, and right to be wrong.
Today, our babies are being raised by babies who have already skipped over God
Today, our children learning the hard way is resulting in death, or a death sentence.
Fights in life are no longer fair
Our children's knowledge of spirituality has sunk to an all-time low
The level has spiked for madness and devastation
Our kids do not understand longsuffering or longevity
If there is no answer to a solution, they think suicide is the way to go.
Poverty is unacceptable to many; however fast money and material riches are not the answer.
Adults should be protecting our children, blood or not, but instead are hustling them!

Our youth are killing, or dying unnecessarily, or being trafficked like human barter.

We owe our children an apology! We dropped the ball! We must take back the reins from the world, instructing our children, **like back in the day,** training them in the way they should go. This is a spiritual battle!

Let's go back to the way we raised our kids like **'back in the day'**, teaching the good news so that we hear and report more good news and see our children in it

Let us change the direction of our children's spiritual growth and life

Let us instruct our children of their true identities and God's real plan for them

Like back in the day.

Chapter 2
To The Fruits

Fruit that can be consumed is usually tasty and succulent, it is also good for the body and refreshing to the soul. There is also other 'fruit' that while it is not edible, reflects characteristics that have been absorbed, in the mind and body and soul, and reflect the type of person you are or have become or are striving to be.

Fruits Intro- (Types of Fruit)

The three main fruits are:

> **Citrus fruits**: such as lemons, limes, oranges & grapefruits, and they contain acid.

> **Non-citrus fruits**: every other fruit including apples, berries, bananas.

> **Dry fruits:** These fruits have lower water ingredient such as figs, dates, raisons, & apricots.

Good Fruit-The best nutritional fruits are:

> Fruits that have **potassium** such as peaches and nectarines. ...

> Fruits that are ***anti-inflammatory*** such as pineapple

> Fruits that are ***good for your heart*** such as grapes

> Fruits that have ***vitamins*** such as kiwi.

Unhealthy Fruits—there are unhealthy fruits that do not have great nutritional value, such as fruit with high sugar or calorie content. These fruits taste great but are not good for diabetics or people with acid reflux. Dried or canned fruits or fruit juice are included in this menu.

Rotten Fruits – Rotten fruits are fruits that have spoiled, beyond the ripe and safe stage to eat. They will literally make you sick and should not be consumed. *Period!*

Fruit of the enemy (Bad Fruit)

Matthew 7 v15 – 20 (Amplified Version)

[15] "Beware of the false prophets, [teachers] who come to you dressed as sheep [appearing gentle and innocent], but inwardly are ravenous wolves. [16] By their fruit you will recognize them [that is, by their contrived doctrine and self-focus]. Do people pick grapes from thorn bushes or figs from thistles? [17] Even so, every healthy tree bears good fruit, but the unhealthy tree bears bad fruit. [18] A good tree cannot bear bad fruit, nor can a bad tree bear good fruit. [19] Every tree that does not bear good fruit is cut down and thrown into the fire. [20] Therefore, by their fruit you will recognize them [as false prophets].

Fruit of God (Good Fruit)

James 3 v17 – 18 KJV

17 But the wisdom that is from above is first pure, then peaceable, gentle, and easy to be intreated, full of mercy and good fruits, without partiality, and without hypocrisy.18 And the fruit of righteousness is sown in peace of them that make peace.

In the word, it says **'you shall know them by their fruits'**. Well, Tree Pears, what do you mean? I'm glad you asked. This means that whatever your walk is, however, you are living, your fruit (characteristics) will show. You will be able to recognize this in others just as they will recognize the fruits in you. If you don't know the Lord, your actions will reflect this in your speech, how you live, and how you treat people.

It doesn't mean that you have a sign on your head, saying 'I am worldly.' Before many of us were born again, we did a lot, remember? Most of us would like to forget what we have done. Of course, there is much that we try to forget, as we should not hold on to the past. Our actions were certainly not all Godly. As a matter of fact, the transition was a slow process.

Before you knew of Christ you had to learn of Him, accept Him in your heart and begin to learn and receive Him and His word, His doctrine, and His kingdom. He may have started working on your heart before you even realized it was Him. We also had to learn and understand 'dying to self, daily' which simply means each new day you live more for and with Christ, as His mercies are new every morning. I'm still standing, but I'm still dying, daily.

We've all been there! If you are lying, cussing, stealing, deceiving, fornicating, perpetrating a fraud, or killing, just to name a few, these characteristics are not good fruits. But God sits high and looks low and has rescued the lowest from the lowest. Boy am I glad!

As you begin to know Christ, your fruits will change from bad to good. You will desire less of the worldly things, as you come to know Christ better. His word will begin to show you just what bearing good fruit means.

Forgiveness is a good fruit. Walking in peace and love is good fruit. Showing compassion is good fruit. Praying for others is good fruit. Sharing your testimony of how Christ changed your life is the fruit of your words. God can change the fruit of the alcoholic, the drug abuser, the prostitute, the liar, the thief, and even sickness and disease, but they must want it. If He knocks on the door of your heart, please let Him in, you won't be disappointed. When your change has become evident, pay it forward and remember to sow the seeds that bear His fruit.

The Fruits of The Spirit

But the fruit of the Spirit is love, joy, peace, patience, kindness, goodness, faithfulness, gentleness, self-control; against such things there is no law.
Galatians 5:22-23

1 Corinthians 13:4-7

Love - *"Love is patient, love is kind. It is not jealous, is not pompous, it is not inflated, it is not rude, it does not seek its own interests, it is not quick-tempered, it does not brood over injury, it does not rejoice over wrongdoing but rejoices with the truth. It bears all things, believes all things, hopes all things, endures all things."*

Psalm 94:18-19

Joy- *"When I say, 'My foot is slipping, 'your mercy, LORD, holds me up. When cares increase within me, your comfort gives me joy."*

Philippians 4:6-7

Peace- *"Have no anxiety at all, but in everything, by prayer and petition, with thanksgiving, make your requests known to God. Then the peace of God that surpasses all understanding will guard your hearts and minds in Christ Jesus."*

2 Peter 3:9

Longsuffering- *"The Lord is not slack concerning His promise, as some count slackness, but is longsuffering toward us, not willing that any should perish but that all should come to repentance."*

Luke 6:35-36

Kindness- *"But rather, love your enemies and do good to them, and lend expecting nothing back; then your* reward will be great, and you will be children of the Most High, for he himself is kind to the ungrateful and the wicked. Be merciful, just as [also] your Father is merciful."

Romans 12:6-8

Goodness- "Since we have gifts that differ according to the grace given to us, let us exercise them: if prophecy, in proportion to the faith; if ministry, in ministering; if one is a teacher, in teaching; if one exhorts, in exhortation; if one contributes, in generosity..." —

Psalm 89:8 KJV

Faithfulness- O Lord God of hosts, Who is a strong Lord like unto thee? Or to thy faithfulness round about thee?

1 Peter 3:15

Gentleness- But in your hearts honor Christ the Lord as holy, always being prepared to make a defense to anyone who asks you for a reason for the hope that is in you; yet do it with gentleness and respect,

Titus 2:11-12

Self-control- For the grace of God has appeared that offers salvation to all people. It teaches us to say "No" to ungodliness and worldly passions, and to live self-controlled, upright and godly lives in this present age..."

I Write

Creatively, excitedly, decidedly, I write.
Expressively, effectively, affectively, I write.
Repeatedly, in spite of me, inspiring me, I write.
Defending me, pretending me, I think and then I write
Writing passionately, even in doubt of me.
Writing spiritually, so very proud of me.
I speak of lessons learned, achievements earned desires
yearned and folks discerned

Its ministry!
I write to calm your stormy sea.
As it ministers to you and me.
I write to change a life and as you say, 'make it plain!',
the better I see.

I write to cross some T's and dot some 'I's.
If I step on your toes, I do apologize.
They say hindsight is 2020. Sometimes I write for the
love of money.
My writing can take you back and move you forward.
Like chess, my writing can check you, and then check
your mate.

My writing can also make better days very appealing.
My words may upset you or hurt your feelings.

If my words hurt your feelings, forgive me this time.
I have words to soothe the heavy in your mind.
My writing is therapy for me and should not bring you
stress,
but only to help you bless and be blessed.
My writing speaks of what I used to seek,
and the God I have now found.

So, my pride I put down
I write to let you know I'm wearing a different crown.
If I smile, laugh, or cry, what better way to express?
Than to write explaining why I may be under duress.
I hope it's about my writing you rave
if it has helped you move from being worldly to saved.

My writing will minister beyond the day I die.
The next time you see my writing, just say 'hi'.
But know that Jesus has the last word and He read me
like a book.
As my words are for Him and I hope to get you hooked.

If You Could Change You

Suppose you could change your looks after birth,
After spending some time on God's precious earth.
Would you accept yourself, just the way that you are?
Would you alter God's property and His work thus far?

Would you keep your same eyes, Your flat nose? Your
long chin?
Would you keep your thick hair or the color of your
skin?
Would you change your complexion to be darker or
lighter?
Would you be black or Asian or your white skin be
whiter?

Would you alter your size, change from fat genes to
thin?
Or from smaller to bigger, now that big girls are in?
Would your IQ go higher working smarter, not harder?
Would you alter your height? Go from short to much
taller?

Would you change your lifestyle from rich living to
poor?
Would you give up good health for the wealth you
adore?
Would you settle to change from a poor life to rich?
Would you alter your ego or become a good witch?

Would you change your small breast, to be large, for a
flirt?
Just to wear a tight shirt, and a harness that hurts.
Men, why alter your manhood to wear skirts and heels?
You should promise yourself there'll be no messy deals!
If I become thin would my heart, shrink too.
Would I stop showing love that I've given to you?

Would my new personality benefit me?
I might become one God's not happy to see.

I might lose my wisdom. My brain might shut down.
Who cares if my eyes are black, green, or brown?
Would you change your mind to become much smarter?
Or prefer to be ignorant so you wouldn't be bothered.

If we alter ourselves, will we then be accepted?
How would they perceive us? They still might reject us.
We are not really sure how a change would affect us.
There's a much better way that I know to perfect us.

We can work on the outside, but what about in?
Fake nails and weave tails don't work under skin.
Would you change your past to avoid new mistakes?
With all that I've mentioned, change needs to take
place.

But God's change is different, accept Jesus inside of you
Please trust and have faith, the Lord will provide for
you.

Your mindset is key for the 'aura' around you.
Place His wisdom before you and Christ will abound
you.

You've heard it before. Your body, God's temple.
How you carry yourself is what sets the example.
Hold your head up high, walk with grace and class.
Please do not throw stones if you live under glass.

If low self-esteem is the problem you're feeling,
Stop knocking yourself and get on with your healing
So let your light shine and keep your mind steady.
When the Lord calls your name, you better be ready.

Folks, please listen carefully. I want you to think
You are all unique, in the word its distinct
When you die to self-daily, you're changing your life.
His good fruit will show as you're living for Christ

Change your mind for the Lord. He will help with your quest.
Say a prayer. Ask for God. He can fill your request.
No one body is perfect. We should all stand apart.
Our God only cares about what's inside of your heart.

You don't have the right to change God's property.
God created this world and He said 'LET' there be.
Change your car, change your house, change your diet or status,
But show people around, you're a blessed 'apparatus'

When you tear yourself down, you create your own problems,
But the Lord will enhance your ability to solve them.
Accept that you're blessed and what God does in you
By the fruit of His word, He is changing me too.

Left for Dead, Right to Life

As I walked along Life's highway on the road to destiny.
Saw directions up ahead but had forgot the Christ in
me.
Tried to focus on the words. Darkness hid them from
the light.
Signs ahead gave me a choice. Left for dead or right to
life?

I saw the signs up on the road saying DETOUR but
disguised.
So I went through some wrong doors, pushing wisdom
to the side.
But I realized my problem as I struggled through this
fight.
This ain't living, I'm a captive. Jesus came to give me
life.

I remember Jesus's miracles in the Bible, souls believed
Raised a widow's son from death, young man spoke
from coffins sleeve.
Raised the 12-year-old young lady with a powerful
command.
Arise! He said; She got up from the touch of Jesus' hand.

There was a woman with an issue, in her life, a bloody
mess.
Twelve whole years she was Uncleanly, had no life and
close to death.
Looking for Him, and she found him. Touched his
garment. She was bold.
Jesus healed her, called her daughter, and her faith, it
made her whole

Lazarus was left for dead. He was buried in the tomb.
Four days he laid behind the stone with stench of

death's perfume.
When Jesus came, He wept, but then cried, 'Lazarus come forth!'
True amazement and belief for all to see, a praise report.

If your way of life is desperate, empty, all alone and drained.
Are you tired, weak, diseased, abused or holding on to pain?
If Jesus said arise and raised believers from the dead,
if Jesus healed some women, some had issues that they dread

If Jesus said, 'Come forth, be loosed, restored, and be renewed.'
If you believe in Him, what do you think he'll do for you?
His story doesn't change for man, child, daughter, or a wife
Left for dead, the wrong direction. Jesus is the right to life.

Life Prolonged

I could not see your face
But I was blinded by your light
I could not hear your words
But the glow within was bright
The closer I became
The sound came forth, the voice so clear
The force was yours to tame
Like a magnet you drew me near

A spirit rare and true
With a heart that shows you care
God has his hand on you
And you determine what to share
You have so much to give
Don't let a doubter steer you wrong
When you live your life for Him
The blessing is a life prolonged.

Lord, Let My Lucy Be

God led me to this church, and I thank God for the connection.
It was me, of little faith, but I was humbled by correction.
To do their job, the ushers said, Miss, move up to the front.
I moved on up to Lucy's side, with Jesus in the hunt.
So overwhelmed with tears, I cried, the whole church could see me.
God comforted my troubled soul, then I met Lucy B!

She handed me some tissues, but I was a nervous wreck
With every song and every word, the tears kept coming back.
As intercessors prayed in tongues, I knew not what to do.
I did not plan to stay here long, but God himself had moved.
She looked concerned, but then she knew and came to me again.
She handed me her number as she shared His fruit within.

She comforted and welcomed me to where I would receive.
The word of God, the Holy Ghost, and newborn air I breathed.
I talked to Lucy on the phone. We learned each other better.
I felt I knew her all along. I'm glad the good Lord led her.
To minister and witness, that is where my faith improved.
She was a devout Christian, and she reached from deep to soothe.

She teased me of my tears, but she knew whence and why I cried.
I told her of my fears, but she saw Jesus on my side.
The *Lord renewed my strength as we both shared our testimony.*
'Be sure to call, Tree anytime!', extending herself to me.
Lucy was a fighter and she shared with me her struggles,
She was such a strong believer that her faith in God had doubled.

For *me, she was so caring, Jesus' kindness I received.*
My first friend at my brand-new home. Her name Is Lucy B!
A spirit bright and lively, and her faith helped me believe.
This poem, for Sister Lucy. Lord, please let my Lucy Be!

(Rest Well, Sister Lucy, Rest Well!)

My Passion For The Poetry

With my passion for the poetry,
I can write when I am wrong, write If I do not belong,
Even write to create a song.

I write of his grace, or a lonely place,
I write of seeking his face, or of troubles in race,
I can write of a notion, or feeling emotion,
While awaiting loves potion, or true love's devotion,
I know this is strange, but I write when deranged,
My whole life has changed, in my poems arranged,
For my world to expand, my words crossing the land,
Poems for a woman or man, words that join lovers'
hands.

I write thanks to my God, while confirming in nod,
That I am on His squad, like two peas in a pod,
All the words may not rhyme, though some quote
paradigms,
Many poems speak of time, ringing bells, like a chime,
When my passion's released, I can write with a peace,
Praising God first, not least, praying problems to cease.

With pure passion as fact, a poem, once a class act,
A cold-hearted attack, or my life back on track,
Before the words I had went from pen to the pad,
They were feelings of pain, an attempt to explain,
Words to fight the insane, while protecting the brain,
But with God I remained, standing tall just the same,
A poem, once a cry, or a life riding high, or a love that
had died, causing many to sigh,
A poem, once a laugh, written on God's behalf, a life
lived too fast, or an era gone past.
A poem, once controlled by a wicked soul, became a
great story told.,
Showed God's love to behold.

Before a poem, words were action, and some attractions or reaction,
Words that spoke of satisfaction. Knowing wealth, I soon would lack none.
A real-life drama written in script, I wrote of my soul restored and stripped.
Like pages in a book. I flipped, I might have tripped or even unzipped,
My mind and spilled my bursting guts, wanting to fuss, I have even cussed,
but writing for life, praise God I must,
With a passion it is poetry or bust!
Before it formed, the poem was words, before the words, the words a thought,
Before the thought, the thought a memory, a passionate way to remember seeing thee,

To reminisce about a kiss or one you have missed, now picture this:
It is a way to express when under stress, write about your mess, or if you've been blessed,
In poetry, I am the scribe, who sets the vibe, as I describe,
A situation that elates, as my soul relates.
In poetry, all the things I write are of life.
Before the words, it was life and before poems, it was words, and before poetry, it was a poem, reflecting the written passion of my life.
Passionately, this poem supports my theory, in expressing the writing of me, there is a passion in living and loving, passionately. I can do all things through Christ Jesus who strengthens me.
To make a difference, I must be actual and factual in teaching and give true testimony as positively and passionately as I can be.
To the world, I introduce me and willingly **my passion for the poetry**.

No Cross, No Crown

One day, in my memory, when I was at work,
While at my computer, my thoughts made me jerk,
I was thinking of Jesus and now energized,
And hearing the gospel, where ministry lies.

How blessed is this music, the gospel, the sound,
Anointed, sweet music that makes me bow down,
Now all understand when they listen and see,
How hearing the gospel is a blessing to me,

The music, so sweet and God in my heart.
Remember, you need Him there, never to part.
With all of the gospel, the old and the new,
There's always a song that will minister to you.

I remember a song that has always been around.
The spiritual's name was No Cross, No Crown.
Whenever I hear it, I now understand
The message composed that has blessed the land.

The message so evident, words were so clear,
You need to have Jesus or judgment you'll fear.
The cross is salvation and heaven your crown.
You must receive Jesus before you're put down.

No matter the song, it's a ministry message
To ensure the deliverance of God holy passage.
We love him. We need him. We praise him today.
Receive His salvation. In Jesus name we pray.

Not Standing Still, But Standing Tall

Your vision, your baby, you cradled it.
Your dream, from hurt, you labeled it.
In rough seas, big waves changed minds.
Searching the waters; help hard to find.

Looking to God, you asked Him, 'Why?'
He said, 'Go forth and don't be shy!'
When you asked why, he said. 'Why ask? '
This dream was no one else's task

For years, this had become your vision,
In going forth, pursuing your mission.
Your ministry gives God the glory,
So, find the souls and tell your story.

Your prayers create a finished work,
As you set free hearts full of hurt,
For how you bless, God blesses, more
You are the key to Safe Harbor's door.

Dedicated to Erica Parker Jordan
Founder of Safe Harbor for Women & Children &
Turning Your Pain to Power Ministries

Safe Harbor

Please find me a Safe Harbor.
Where I can drop my worries and woes.
Please find me a Safe Harbor
Where I can shed my heavy clothes.

Please show me a safe haven
Where I can lay my weary head.
Please find me a Safe Harbor
Where there is always an open bed.

Please show me an alternative
Where I don't know the word abuse.
Please give me an ear to hear **me**
Where no one calls my words 'excuse'.

Please find a heart to hold me
Where there's no room to close the door.
Please find arms to console me
Where God's real love shows even more.

Please send me a safe haven
Be I, woman, child, or girl.
Please place me with your protection.
So I'm not wandering in this world.

Please show me that I can find love.
So, I'll know fate if my heart bleeds.
Please find me a Safe Harbor
Where angels come and hear my needs.

Please find me a Safe Harbor
Where there is prayer, and I am healed.
Please rescue me from my torture.
My problems root can be revealed.

Please find me a safe haven
Where no one faults me for the truth.
Please find me a Safe Harbor
Where better 'Me's can be produced.

The Five Folders

The love for our ministers is deeply instilled.
We honor Five Folders, so spiritually filled.
They have ministered greatly to all who will listen
Kingdom content, with God's intent, it is divine
medicine

The doctrine of Jesus puts change within reach.
As we search for the truth while they speak, preach, or
teach.
They have gathered the people for multiple reasons.
To sow kingdom seeds and unleash a new season.

Their words remove doubt, building strong confidence.
They are builders for God teaching faith's evidence.
The words they deliver has changed our lives.
As we listen to what our Five-Folders provide.

Their prayers have touched us, spiritually,
As they teach restoration, we are captives set free
Through obedience and even their own sacrifice
We're in awe of the teaching, as it changes our life

Five folders exhort and pray without ceasing
They incorporate prayer as our faith is increasing
Removing the doubt with a Holy Ghost teaching
The lesson is Jesus, whose life was redeeming

They have nurtured us, coached us, and mentored us
too.
They have buried us, married us, and prayed souls
renewed
They have christened our children and challenged
contenders.
They have counselled the Saints not to be God
offenders.

They have visions & dreams, and we are not excluded.
We are kingdom ambassadors who God has included
They have taught us the word to make better decisions.
They have taught us to plan and prepare for our vision

Apostles, Pastors, Prophets, Teachers, and Evangelists.
*They were **sent** for our lives, so therefore we are blessed*
They have helped us to focus and learn the Word, smarter.
Their guidance allows us to dream even harder

They have taught us to thrive, to become royal rulers
They have taught kingdom wisdom to help with our future
They have taught us to know Matthew 6:33
I must thank you, five folders, for covering me!

Chapter 3
Becoming

And the Lord God said, Behold, the man is become as one of us, to know good and evil: and now, lest he put forth his hand, and take also of the tree of life, and eat, and live forever: **Genesis 3:22**

Becoming- Intro

Becoming: Something that looks good on a person. A correct look or statement: Any process of change for the better.

The Best definition- Any change that involves realizing who you need to be, bringing yourself from a lower state into a better state of mind to focus and live better.One thing I realized about 'becoming' is that a person will need to overcome certain situations in their life to become who God wants them to be.

In this chapter, the poems and Stoetries I have written about are situations I have overcome or experienced overcoming through others in order for a life to change for Christ. Read on.

After The Wedding, The Marriage

There was a wedding.
It was planning and spending, and more planning.
We decided we would do the right thing by God and for Christ.
We decided we were going to do ministry with each other
We were saying 'we will work together' and let no 'thing' break us up.
Our 'vow' was to be a threesome, Him, Myself and God.
We called our 'families' to be a part of our special day
I bought a beautiful dress, costing hundreds, no less.
Counseled, and covered by the prayer warriors, as we remembered to pray.
Our special day finally arrived.
It was beautiful. He looked so handsome, in his tuxedo.
Of course, there were the few small problems,
But, overall, it was a joyous occasion.
There were the tears, the party, the food, the reunions,
The congratulations and the lying,
Or should I say, 'tall tales being spun'.
The dancing, oh yes, the dancing!
It was bittersweet and sunshine.
What we never considered was
After the wedding, the marriage.
The marriage as new and newlyweds.
The children, the stepchildren, the bills.
The loss of income. The sicknesses. The tiredness.
The ministry in the marriage.
The marriage and the ministry. The doubts?
The spiteful prayers, asking God to fix what was not fair.
The backsliding! The attacks. (The enemy hates marriage.)
The not cheating while feeling cheated.
The marriage seeing bad habits repeated.

The marital frustrations? The spousal remorse!
'I should have just stayed by myself!' LOL!
The marriage sometimes lifeless, sometimes loveless.
sometimes moneyless.
Seeing no light at the end of the tunnel.
But inviting God to step in, together, repenting,
rebuking, re-learning, accepting,
Allowing the laying on of Holy hands.
The marriage with the counseling, support, new life,
new hope, new vision, new love.
The marriage now under God's umbrella,
The marriage with the promise to love one another,
unconditionally.
The promise to correct ourselves and make it work.
The marriage, balanced by God, not 50/50 but 100/100.
Lord, enlarge our marital territory.
Bless our marriage, indeed.
Teach us to love ourselves so we can love each other,
better!
Teach me not to hurt him with my words.
Teach him to be more understanding of my needs.
Teach us to build this union into a lifetime of positive
togetherness.
Allow our times of loving in intimacy to be like fire,
more love, more joy.
Now two, united in ministry as one for God in Jesus'
name
Together we pray, and it is so, Amen!

All I Can Say

Where did He find such a spirit'
so beautiful and bright
Where did he find such a twinkle?
That would sparkle day or night
Where did he find such a true heart?
That would make a flower bloom
Where did he find such a sunbeam?
That would brighten up a room
Only in you could he find this
He has blessed you more than you know
Your smile like a sparkle of diamonds
And your gleam has an afterglow
Anointed with such a true spirit
Your darkness now brighter than days
Your presence uplifts and endears me
I love you, that's all I can say

Dedicated to my granddaughter,
Tejsia Ayahnna Gladden

Be Ready

Believe

> in God, He is real, and He is worthy

Expect

> the unexpected, we know we are going to pass on, but we don't know when or how

Receive

> His word, it is the instructions for your life

Elevate

> your level of faith

Accept

> Him into your heart, He is already knocking, you must open the door

Decide

> for yourself to know Him, when there is no one else, He is there for you

Yes, Say YES! to God's will

Be Ready!

"But forget all that—it is nothing compared to what I am going to do. For I am about to do something new. See, I have already begun! Do you not see it? I will make a pathway through the wilderness. I will create rivers in the dry wasteland. **Isaiah 43:18–19 (NLT)**

Clean Out Your Closet

If there is one thing in my house that I don't look forward to, it's cleaning out my closets. They call it spring cleaning. De-cluttering in our living space is important. So is a de-cluttering of the mind.

When we go through our closets, it is always a slow process because we start finding things that have been buried, covered up, boxed in, thrown to the back and just forgotten. The problem is, it's an item that you don't need, still in your closet, taking up space. Until you do something about it, you won't have space for anything fresh and new.

Why do we hold on to the old stuff?

Many things are appliances that no longer work, clothes that are too large or small, but are just too good to throw away, or things that should have been tossed way back when, like the old bomb we used to smoke weed out of, oh, don't forget the joint roller. Yeah! Act like you don't remember that one. And those good old sex toys from our wild and kinky days.

Don't play yourself. If you don't know God at this point, these things are not what you need. If you do know God, or are a new believer why are you keeping these things? Were you holding on to them as keepsakes for your children or grandchildren? I don't think so. Then, there are the pictures of the old boyfriends or girlfriends, all of the 'ex's.

Question, is 'ex' still marking the spot? *Oh, what memories do we keep?* 'I remember the way he used to.... I remember the way she used to...', you fill in the blanks. Question? Are you married now? Are you saved? Are those old pictures of your husband or your wife? If they are not, then why are you keeping these memories? You don't want to forget the old times, but here is a word of advice, **forget the old times**, and get ready for the time of your life.

Throw the old mess out!

What folks do not realize is that the enemy and memories go hand in hand. I'm not talking about the good memories. Thank God for every beautiful memory, like the sound of a child laughing, or wonderful wedding you attended, or our relatives, living and deceased. Nothing can replace those memories, they are keepers!

I am talking about the things that we hold onto that will do us no good in the future but *will not let us let go of the past*. There are old, haunting memories that bring painful reminders. Can't you just hear the sound of the wicked laughter? Many of us need to take the time to do a spring cleaning of the mind. A de-cluttering is necessary.

I want you to pretend you have a wastebasket next to you and think of what is in your mind that you have been holding on to, that you need to forget because it has been holding you back, keeping you from going forward and from becoming who God wants you to be. Or better yet, get a real wastebasket, and a small pad and pen. Start tossing these things that have been cluttering up your mind and life for the longest time. Write each negative thing down, then throw it in the basket. *You have got to make a decision to let it go!* The hurtful memories that have been boxed in, covered up, and thrown to the back must be thrown out! They are hindering your footsteps, your progress, and your future. With that wastebasket next to you, and your eyes closed, just began to toss stuff in the basket, piece by piece, hurt by hurt, old pain. after old pain.

Have a funeral for the mess!

Before you realize it, your basket will be full. You'll say, wow, I didn't know I had so much junk in there. My mind was jacked up. *It's time to get the Jack out of your mind.*

Here's another exercise for you. Pick a day, any day, to have a release party and just begin to write about what's been holding you back. Speak about it; whether you are talking to someone or talking to God, get some 3 by 5 cards and on each one list an old haunting memory and then **make a decision to have a funeral,** and bury the negative stuff. Pray about it and ask the Lord for forgiveness for others and most importantly yourself. But once you have thrown it out, it's out of your mind, forever! **DON'T FIND A REASON TO KEEP IT OR BRING IT BACK.**

Do not store hurtful things from the past in your mind that can hinder your future. Realize this, just like a day of spring cleaning, when you are finished sweating, separating, tossing, sweeping, mopping and dusting, you can see progress and space. The closet smells fresh, and so does the whole room. You're ready to open your blinds and windows and let the fresh air in.

You won't care if anyone looks in because you have nothing to hide anymore. After cleaning out the closet of your mind, you will feel the same way. Your mind will feel pounds lighter and there will be room to grow. Burdens will be lifted from your shoulders.

You'll be able to walk with a different gate and show that nothing can break your stride, or hold you down, because the closets of your mind has been cleaned. Halleluiah!

Do not be yoked together with unbelievers. For what do righteousness and wickedness have in common? Or what fellowship can light have with darkness? 2 **Corinthians 6:14 (NLT)**

Equally Yoked

*In my new walk with Christ, didn't know what it meant
To be equally yoked. I have since to repent.
When we started dating, 'yoked' had just been explained.
We thought we were ok and loving the same
I was just being taught of the rules of God's game
While loving my new life in Jesus Christ name.
My partner and I still had the same goals
To live life for Christ in mind, body, and soul.
God's commandments, not always so clear to understand
That when bonding together as woman and man,
You cannot make plans for another individual
To change their life to fit your version of spiritual.
Lest you may discover they are not ready yet.
Don't take on the gamble just to win a bet.
If you or your mate are avoiding the devil
Being equally yoked, is being on the same level.
If its marriage you want, but your mate is not saved,
Invite Christ's counsel so you don't get played.
If you are both saved but with different rules,
You'll be wasting much time, until you've been schooled.*

*Both, Walking in love, the WORD must be adored
When you love God in marriage, He becomes your core.
You should love God first while you love your mate too,
Reject worldly ideas you may think to be cool.
The controlling factors that are wrong for the soul,
The unclean habits that have long become old.
But what do you do when the vows have been said?*

You may think it's too late when you're moving ahead.
If you both love the Lord, do you worship alone?
Is it just you in church while your mate is at home?
Partake in good counseling to learn of your faults.
Receive some true ministering before cutting them off.
If the bond with your partner is not what you've heard
You both must be yoked, *giving love God prefers.*
You pray for the love, you pray for the marriage,
You pray for salvation, and both be encouraged.
Remember that when you're united, as one
The marriage needs work it is not just all fun.
Pray on your union it's never a joke.
You both need the WORD to be equally yoked

Get Up

Beloved, how is your life? Is your happiness gone?
Are you in **your** house? Is **your** light turned on?
Do you face each day with a feeling of dread?
Is your spirit drained? Are you living dead?

Don't you think it's time that you fill your cup?
No more drowning in sorrow; wake your dead self up!
All it takes is a word for you to believe,
Expand your capacity and prepare to receive.

Hear a word from the Lord and receive it yourself.
Stop looking for words that bless someone else.
Know that God is a keeper and deliverer, to.
Just believe in His promises. He'll take care of you.

Keep walking in him and receiving his power.
We are children of God walking under his tower.
As a witness for Christ, teach faith to believe.
Stick and stay in His light and the more you'll receive.

When you speak of his goodness. Don't expect a revival,
Tell all who are listening why you read the Bible.
From a tiny word spoken like a mere mustard seed.
Rays of LIFE grow your faith as a seed grows a tree.

Crucified, on the cross, Jesus died for all sins.
Buried three long days, yet He rose once again.
He is the living water, drink the word without fuss.
Let the dead things go. Hear His word and **Get Up!**

Girl, Get Up!: *It's The Remix*

Discover your **Untapped Potential**.
Forget who you thought you were, so you can be who God wants you to be.

Nehemiah 8:10 (KJV) **"Do not be grieved, for the joy of the Lord is your strength".**

Psalms 28:7 **"The Lord is my strength and my shield; in him my heart trusts."**

Isaiah 40:31 **"But those who wait for the Lord shall renew their strength, they shall mount up with wings like eagles, they shall run and not be weary, they shall walk and not faint."**

Philippians 4:13 **"I can do all things through him who strengthens me."**

2 Corinthians 12: 9-10 **"My grace is sufficient for you, for power is made perfect in weakness."**

Jeremiah 29:11 **"For surely I know the plans I have for you, says the Lord, plans for your welfare and not for harm, to give you a future with hope."**

Isaiah 30:18 **"Therefore, the Lord waits to be gracious to you; therefore, he will rise up to show mercy to you."**

1 Peter 5:7 **"Cast all your anxiety on him, because he cares for you."**

Psalm 27:14 **"Wait for the Lord; be strong, and let your heart take courage; wait for the Lord!"**

Micah 7:7 **"But as for me, I will look to the Lord, I will wait for the God of my salvation; my God will hear me."**

Romans 8: 24-25 **"For in hope we were saved. Now hope**

that is seen is not hope. For who hopes for what is seen? But if we hope for what we do not see, we wait for it with patience."

Girl, Get UP! (Tap into your **U**ntapped **P**otential)

So, you walk into a room; you have your guard up
Your spirit's filled with gloom; pain tore your heart up
There's no prayers or intercession, where's your worship?
Daughter, He's the living water; quench your thirst up!

You keep crying to the Lord, bring your esteem up!
With faith and trust in him you can redeem up
Your voice should never waiver, daughter, speak up!
By now your kingdom growth should tear defeat up

You're not tore up from the floor up, time to clean up
You are blessed and highly favored, build your Queen up
You're a gift, as it was Christ who gave his life up
With His blood, He paid the price, and then He went up

The word provides the answers if you listen up
Your confidence will shine & doubt will lessen up
Strength & Faith and fear of God will help you rise up
Study! Show thyself approved and dry your eyes up!

Put a smile upon your face, go on get dressed up
If you really love the Lord, you better 'Fess Up
Stop you're crying, God is calling you to man up!
You can RISE above your issues, so, Girl, Get Up!
Girl, Get Up!

I will give thanks and praise to You, for I am fearfully and wonderfully made; Wonderful are Your works, And my soul knows it very well. **Psalm 139:14 –Amplified Bible**

God Inside

*No longer can my spirit hide
My faith, my love, the God inside.
In his own image, God made man.
To know I am that, that I am.
We search for God, His reign we seek
And righteously, His words we speak*

*God's word I eat and drink thy cup
Just pack my soul. Lord, fill me up.
Just stuff me full, till I explode.
Through righteous words, I will implode.
Anointed, with my Kingdom pride
Lord, let it show, the God inside.*

For this reason, I am telling you, whatever things you ask for in prayer [in accordance with God's will], believe [with confident trust] that you have received them, and they will be given to you. **Mark 11:24**

A Reason to Believe

God has given me. A reason to believe.
Through Christ, it is the word that I receive.
Through prayer, it is the way that I retrieve.
Through my mind, it is the way that I conceive

Through love, it is the way that I reach out.
Through comfort, it's the way to stop the doubt.
Through praise, the name of Jesus I call out
Through Christ, I am a Christian who's devout

God Is My Slomin Shield
(Slomin Shield© is a brand name Home Security Alarm system)

"But be sure of this, that if the head of the house had known at what time the thief was coming, he [would have been awake and alert, and] would not have allowed his house to be broken into."
Luke 12:39 (Amplified Bible)

"By this I know that You favor and delight in me, because my enemy does not shout in triumph over me."
Psalm 41:11 (Amplified Bible)

The enemy's goal is to upset your soul
While he poisons your family and your household
He's a predator, burglar, murderer, thief
His plan is to grant you no sleep, and no peace

As the enemy breaks in and enters your home
We must prepare to protect our family, our throne
With spiritual preparation and our minds intact
Mother's, put your guard up against his attack

Oh, he will find a way to sneak into your house
Through any crevice, crack or chimney, no doubt
If we are women of God, who are protecting our offspring
We want the same for our loved ones, not an enemy offering

Enemy, at one time, you caused so much pain
By my tears, sickness, and sorrow, somehow you gained
You took away my job, but God taught me to see
For me to prove my love, he used the enemy

You turned my child away from me, I loved her just the same

I always claim her soul, and that's my prayer in Jesus'
name
The bishop prophesied, but family members still died
My daughter said goodbye, my grand said, 'grandma
why?'

It was too easy to cry but God was on my side
I could have lived a lie or not just even tried
You vowed my husband yours, regardless of his fight
But I must laugh at you because you're wrong, God's
right

I'm no longer afraid, I will stand up to you
You stick to slimy things; I stick to God like glue
I am the mother, castle keeper, and queen of my throne
As God's assistant, I'm the (s.o.u.l.) soul protector of my
home

My family knows me as the (h.m.i.c.) head mother in
charge
There is no way I'll let you reign in my house, living
large
We pray for all around us, God's praise comes through
my mouth
As I rebuke the ugly demons with a righteous praise and
shout

There's no negotiating when Satan's crew is about
The welcome mat is lifted, so get out of my house.
I am determined melancholy will not claim this territory
In my home and in this house, there will be a Jesus
story
The enemy comes, you heard it, to steal, kill, and
destroy
But not in my house, enemy, not anymore
God is my **Slomin Shield,** believe me, there's no doubt
Some may not know it yet, but I am a Jesus scout

Uncle Sam, he did not want me, but God was ready for me
I enlisted in His army, and I gave Him all the glory
I became one of His warriors, fighting, praying to save souls
I became a spiritual trooper, as I loosened Satan's hold

He has tampered with my loved ones, hiding behind enemy lines
Hiding from God's angels, until a wounded soul he finds
No remorse in the devil's attacks, slaying all from human to cattle
Jesus had me on the front line, now I'm ready for this battle

Mothers', don't stop praying, we must build our ammunition
We must use our Godly weapons and expose the sick conditions
When we worship and we pray, throwing mud in the enemy's face
We make the devil madder, calling God from our secret place

When you stand up to the enemy he shrinks before your eyes
He supports the wrong, but you take charge to cast out all the lies
No more ill will, non-believing, and most of all no doubt
No reversal of what God did, in Jesus' name, Get satan out!

Moms, protect your house, protect your home, don't forget the oil
You must fight for God on Gods behalf and labor in His soil

Be obedient and spread Gods word, witness, and confess
Dance on the devil's playground and lessen up your stress

I've tried to give instruction, Moms, on battling the devil
The enemy is low, and we stand higher on Gods level
You must claim your souls and claim your home and let your faith reveal

I have shown the troll the exit, cause God is my **Slomin Shield**!

God's Following Me

Sometimes I want to laugh out loud.
I'm so silly!
I know I can't outrun the clouds,
Clouds following me.
Sometimes I want to skip along.
Oh, that's silly!
Instead, I sing a blues filled song.
Pain following me.
Why? Oh, why does it hurt so much inside?
When life is not right, day is now night and hope is out of sight.
Why? Oh, why do I hide in shame?
When my world is insane,
I must refrain from claiming the pain!
Sometimes I want to laugh out loud.
I'm so silly.
I need to tell my past goodbye.
Past following me.
Sometimes I want to skip along.
Oh, that's silly.
Instead, I sing a better song.
God's following me.

God's Word on Your Potential

Hebrews 11:6

⁶ But without faith it is impossible to please him: for he that cometh to God must believe that he is, and that he is a rewarder of them that diligently seek him.

Genesis 1:26–27

²⁶ And God said, **let us make man in our image, after our likeness**: and let them have dominion over the fish of the sea, and over the fowl of the air, and over the cattle, and over all the earth, and over every creeping thing that creepeth upon the earth.

²⁷ So God created man in his own image, in the image of God created he him; male and female created he them.

²⁸ And God blessed them, and God said unto them, be fruitful, and multiply, and replenish the earth, and subdue it: and have dominion over the fish of the sea, and over the fowl of the air, and over every living thing that moveth upon the earth.

You have the POTENTIAL to be in God's class. Well in most classes, you have to qualify to be accepted in a class. God has already qualified and accepted us by making us in His image. So, the potential to be is Spirit, and because we have been made in His image, we have the potential to operate like God. **We have his DNA**. Notice it says to operate like God, not as God. Man was the first clones, operating like God but not as God. Look at how creative God was, using all of His potential to create man in every shape, size, and nationality. We don't have all of His abilities, but the potential he has provided allows us capabilities to do many things when we use it.

God has already given you the potential to be fruitful & multiply. So how do you know that you have all of this potential? Because you are only doing a small

percentage of things in life that you want to do.
You have ideas that have not manifested yet. That's potential. If there were no ideas, no thoughts, no desires your minds would be blank. So, imagine that everything that we are manifesting currently, he already gave us the potential to do, and so much more. You should be writing down your ideas, visions and dreams and place them where you can see them, you will eventually start checking the list off, seeing things accomplished.

Its like we have to wake ourselves up and stop sleeping on our own abilities and capabilities.

Genesis 11 v 6

[6] *And the Lord said, Behold, the people is one, and they have all one language; and this they begin to do: and now nothing will be restrained from them, which they have imagined to do.*

God didn't stop the men from building a tower by cutting off there potential, but he confused their language

God is saying that you have the ability to do anything you put your mind to, but this is for good and can also be for evil if that's where your mind is, potential is potential. Make sure your potential is used for the good of man and to represent God and the kingdom.

Mark 9:23 *All things are possible for them that believe. With Faith you can believe your ideas into a reality.*

Psalm 119 v89 *Your word O Lord is eternal; it stands firm in the heavens.*

Our God given potential even includes the ability to influence physical and spiritual matter.

Influence is part of our potential gifting. If I can help you look better, think better, create better, learn of the kingdom of Christ, I am using my potential gifting of influence. If I don't use it, it remains untapped. Tell your neighbor tap in, don't tap out. We even have influence in Heaven. This blew my mind. You have the power to loose on earth and in heaven and you have the power to influence on earth and in Heaven.

Our potential is unlimited on one condition, if you abide in Christ and His words abide in you. We must follow His doctrine, plain and simple. He will give you the desires of your heart as long as they are in conjunction with the desires of his heart and you function in the purpose, He has provided for you. Jesus wants to knock the limits off your mind, but His requirement is that we stay in the word, abide in Him, give Him back His word, have faith to do greater works, trust Him so He can trust us and have faith in us, and He wants us to ask Him of our desires, believe me He will judge if it is under the conditions He's set, and if we are deserving. Maximize your true potential by staying connecting to God.

When God said let us make man in our own image, after our likeness, notice the word 'us' and 'our'. This is plural. I going to call them Team Trinity, the Father, the son & the Holy Spirit. Team Trinity was already in agreement with making us qualified and accepted in their class.

How dare us shrug off the given potential from God. Our potential begins as untapped, but it is not to remain untapped. He has given us a whole life to do something with our God Given potential.

When God made you in His likeness, He didn't make you to look like Him. He made you to **function** like Him. Remember the song from schoolhouse rock, conjunction junction, what's your function?

Function:

Noun- *an activity or purpose natural to or intended for a person or thing.*

Verb - **work or operate in a proper or particular way**.

God has a purpose and if we function like Him, we already have a purpose. With the creation of Adam & Eve He was expecting them/us to operate the same as Him, with purity & sinless.

If you are not operating like God, you are malfunctioning, well unfortunately with Adam and Eve there was a malfunction. Thank God for plan B, Jesus Christ the 2nd Adam.

God functions by faith, so He has faith in Himself and in us, and he has provided you with faith and expects you to execute and activate your faith in Him as he is operating in Faith for you. Faith and trust go together and its factors of the function of the potential he has given us. Hebrews 11 v6 says, without Faith it is impossible to please God. Got Faith? Our potential needs faith!

God sees in you the Potential to dominate,

The potential to rule,

And the potential to subdue the whole earth.

He is already letting us know that we are capable of being leaders and taking charge.

God created you to rule.

RULE

R- REIGN

U- UPHOLD

L- LEAD

E- EMPOWER

Stop living below your privilege. Imagine what God is thinking. He gave us these bodies, and because of sin now dominating so many, people are filling their bodies with junk that God never intended for their bodies. People are claiming things that God never intended them to claim. Folks are worshipping false idols, there's diviners, sorcery, astrology, none of this God intended for us. God called you to dominate and rule with purity and faith. He didn't call you to be a zodiac sign. You're not a Gemini, you're not an Aries, you are a child of the Most High, an ambassador of the Kingdom.

We are to rule over the earth, the earth is not to rule over us. That's a mighty powerful gift that God gave us. The main gift is the Potential he gave us, and within that gift, there are so many more. We are loaded and we need to stop playing. Realize your God given Potential.

I Give What I Live

I could try to sound deep,
Expressing myself with big words that sound
Radically put together in a sentence.
At the end, will you understand what I just said?
I could be short and sweet with words that rhyme.
At the end will you get the point?
At the end, you should get the point, and understand
where I've been,
Where I am, and where I intend to go.

I try to change my style of writing,
So the sound of rhyme is not the same,
The number of verses may change.
The rhythm is not so mundane,
The truth of the matter is.
My words are my truth
It's a true rhyme, it's a life's rhyme,
It's a look at me now, living proof rhyme
Whatever you hear, the message should be made clear
My words cannot be a burden to your sensitive ear
I give what I live
I live what I have learned
I share what I have dared,
I express that I am blessed.

I Said I Do, But Now I Don't

I said I do, but now I don't
I said I would, but now I won't
I said I can, but now I can't
I used to whisper, now I rant

I thought them right, but I was wrong
Soul ties I had, but now they're gone
I said I do, and did again
I lost so much, but now I win

I thought the words, but could not write
Some books are written, not in sight
Christ won the battle, Satan lost the fight
I'm back to claim my true birthright

I've lived a lie, His word was truth
But wounds can heal, I'm living proof
Took back my youth, as I grow older
I used to hide, but now I'm bolder

Accepting Christ, receiving salvation
Has changed my focus, and spiritual station
Yes, I was lost, but now I'm found
I picked up Christ, put Satan down!

Let Me tell you About of Man

Hear my words, wherever you can
I'm here to tell you about a man.
He changed my world from death to life
He rescued me from tear filled nights

This Holy man who changed my ways
Removed the gloom, He heard my praise
I thought I couldn't, He said, 'You can!'
I'm here to share with you that man

He gave his life for you and I
That's why I worship Him on high
He shed His blood on cavalry
Because of Him I've been set free

He is a man I came to know
From Him, His living waters flow
He set me free, He changed my Life
That God filled man is Jesus Christ.

Oil & Water

Oil & Water tried to mix
But Oil was just too slick!
Water thought Oil was smooth
Like the element. He was crude, but never rude.
His seductive voice thwarted her choice
His smile & cologne apprehended her spirit,
Although, like Eve with the serpent,
She should NOT have been near it,
Oil presented to her his slimy character.

Even at the sight of his dark, shiny skin
Water, attracted to her opposite, turned on like a
faucet.
Running hot, always wet, warm in the middle, but cold
in the end.
To him, she was a fresh drink of water,
But He could never be 'Watered Down'.
She was always pouring into him yet being constantly
drained.

His slickness was all he offered, for her there was no
gain
Love was already slippery when they met
While his being attracted her
His way of life distracted her
She did not reign; love was not heaven sent
Water was just a trophy at every event.

It was not a smooth ride, more like a back slide
Often, she cried! His arrogant truth never lied.
In fact, his slim-i-ness 'stained' Water's worth.
He was always slipping, and she, always dripping in
fears and tears
As he became the slickster that tricked her,
Pretending to love.

On the checklist he did not fit 'all of the above'
He was a bad night to Water's good day
Sadly, Oil never planned to stay
His elements, never a complement to her moisture
She had refused to believe his past,
and that their mixture would not last
Now, her doubts of their future thickening.
The acts of their present, sickening.
He was of the world. She, wanting ministry.
Realized there was no chemistry.
She finally understood the formula,
Oil & Water would never mix
'Cause Oil was just too slick.

WHAT HAVE YOU DONE
FOR YOUR 'SELF' LATELY?

What is the purpose of 'SELF'?

> To groom yourself for Christ & the Kingdom...

Strengthen, Edify, Live Life & Forgive.

S -Strengthen

As woman we need to strengthen ourselves spiritually, submit to the word, the more you know of the Christ and the kingdom, the more you grow in the kingdom.

E- Edify

By hearing and receiving the word of the Kingdom of Christ, our souls are being edified and equipped.

L – Live Life

(*Are you really living or just existing?*) We Need to be dying to live and not living to die. Stop denying yourself the pleasures of life because of all the responsibilities that we have or have taken on.

F – Forgive

Have you forgiven your-SELF for past issues?

Luke 9:23 *And he said to them all, if any man will come after me, let him **deny** himself, and take up his cross daily, and follow me.*

First, we must Die to SELF, in order to get our SELF in order

Martha & Mary

Luke 10:38-42 *Now it came to pass, as they went, that he entered into a certain village: and a certain woman named Martha received him into her house. And she had a sister called Mary, which also sat at Jesus' feet, and heard his word. But Martha was cumbered about much serving, and came to him, and said, Lord, dost thou not care that my sister hath left me to serve alone? bid her therefore that she help me. And Jesus answered and said unto her, Martha, Martha, thou art careful and troubled about many things: But one thing is needful: and Mary hath chosen that good part, which shall not be taken away from her.*

We're busy women, always doing things for everybody or every cause, with a to do list. but too often we forget to make ourselves the 'thing to do' or 'put ourselves on the list.'.

By making Jesus and His word our priority, we are on the road to **SELF** recovery by continually learning, praying, worshipping & honoring Him.

So, while we can't help but be like Martha sometimes, we can't forget that at times, we need to be like Mary, not being lazy at all but resting at Jesus feet, gleaning from his presence and word, Strengthening, Edifying, Living & Forgiving - SELF.

A Virtuous Woman (Analyzed)

Proverbs 31 v 10–31 (KJV)

[10] Who can find a virtuous woman? for her price is far above rubies. **(She is /We are - valuable)**

[11] The heart of her husband doth safely trust in her, so that he shall have no need of spoil.

[12] She will do him good and not evil all the days of her life.

(She will not betray her husband; she will have his back)

[13] She seeketh wool, and flax, and worketh willingly with her hands. **(She is/We are creative)**

[14] She is like the merchants' ships; she bringeth her food from afar.

[15] She riseth also while it is yet night, and giveth meat to her household, and a portion to her maidens. **(She/We makes sure our families & others are fed)**

[16] She considereth a field, and buyeth it: with the fruit of her hands she planteth a vineyard. **(She/We worked, toiled, sold and then invested the money)**

[17] She girdeth her loins with strength, and strengtheneth her arms. **(She is/We are not weak)**

[18] She perceiveth that her merchandise is good: her candle goeth not out by night. **(She/We makes sure that everything is in good working order)**

[19] She layeth her hands to the spindle, and her hands hold the distaff. **(She is/We are crafty, constantly working)**

[20] She stretcheth out her hand to the poor; yea, she reacheth forth her hands to the needy. **(She is/We are always helping someone)**

²¹ She is not afraid of the snow for her household: for all her household are clothed with scarlet. **(In the cold she is/we are prepared to make sure her family is warm)**

²² She maketh herself coverings of tapestry; her clothing is silk and purple. **(She is/We are Crafty -enterprising)**

²³ Her husband is known in the gates, when he sitteth among the elders of the land. **(He is recognized as her husband & she is acknowledged)**

²⁴ She maketh fine linen, and selleth it; and delivereth girdles unto the merchant.

²⁵ Strength and honour are her clothing; and she shall rejoice in time to come.

²⁶ She openeth her mouth with wisdom; and in her tongue is the law of kindness. **(People value her words and wisdom)**

²⁷ She looketh well to the ways of her household, and eateth not the bread of idleness. **(She's not lazy, every minute of her day is accounted for)**

²⁸ Her children arise up, and call her blessed; her husband also, and he praiseth her. **(She means the world to her family)**

²⁹ Many daughters have done virtuously, but thou excellest them all.

³⁰ Favour is deceitful, and beauty is vain: but a woman that feareth the Lᴏʀᴅ, she shall be praised. **(She/We fear the Lord)**

³¹ Give her of the fruit of her hands; and let her own works praise her in the gates. **(Her creations and deeds are worthy for her use as well as others)**

As a woman we can be all these things, have an agenda and an itinerary, busy busy, busy being a Martha, but at some point, we need to take the time & lay ourselves down at Jesus feet and be a Mary. Rest the body & mind

& hear & receive His word. This will Strengthen us, Equip & edify us, allow us to Live life better according to the kingdom, and to Forgive ourselves & others as we receive forgiveness from the Father, himself.

Suppose someone asked me to pray

When I first became saved, I loved to hear the already saved women pray. Before and after every meeting and at the beginning of service, they would ask someone to pray.

I was always afraid that someone was going to ask me to pray. I could only remember that some of the women prayed long and hard. It was like fire and brimstone prayers in which you just know that God heard their prayers, and their prayers would be answered.

But as I grew in the Lord, I kept trying to prepare myself as I knew one day it would be my turn. I had to ask the Lord what I would pray for, and how should I pray. He gave me some simple answers. This poem is about that conversation with God.

Suppose someone asked me to pray
Dear Lord, tell me what I would say
unlike others I'm shy, if I give it a try
will my prayers be received the same way?
Lord, please tell me how I should begin
Will my prayer be received from within?
As I give You the glory, if I think you'll ignore me
I may quickly say Amen
Jesus answers in yet a soft voice
Pray for souls to know me and rejoice
Pray for strength and endurance for love and
perseverance
And pray sin is no longer a choice
Remember when praying for souls
You can pray that they are not controlled
For all ask forgiveness and also repentance
as blessings begin to unfold

For Leaders, pray for their well-being
For their families, their coming and leaving
Pray abundance and strength and their family be
blessed!
It's from them you're receiving His great teaching

At last, if you don't get the picture
You do not have to quote every scripture
Just pray for faith building then pray that God's willing
To save you from things that will tempt you
Remember to pray for what ails you, and for what ails
the other Saints too
Rebuke all those demons in the holy name of Jesus
And pray that mindsets be improved
Last pray for the churches upgrade
Then pray that the tithes can be paid

As you pray for all healing, all strength and well-being
Say Amen and be blessed you have prayed
As you become stronger in prayer
You will pray and it won't matter where
You will speak prayer directly on all that affects thee
You'll know Christ's love you will share.

For the earnest expectation of the creature waiteth for the manifestation of the sons of God. **Romans 8:19 KJV**

The Blessing

God said, 'It is finished!'. So, you must not wonder!
It is in the Lords hands, and He will not blunder.
Life requires NOW faith, so please pull your faith out.
It is God you should fear, but don't worry or doubt.

Yes, you may have concerns, but the Father is near
He is hearing your prayers, you have been in His ear
Prayer is the right thing; it is what you should do.
The Lord never tires of hearing from you.

Through doing the word, with much supplication
Christ in us, the hope of glory, we have earnest
expectations
His message is clear as we learn to repent
When God speaks in your life, it may come from one
sent

God knows the results; He is waiting for you.
Believe in His power, in all that you do
Because of His glory, your focus has changed.
Expect the Lord's blessing, keep trusting His name.

The Credit

To whom should I give the credit??
When trouble is knocking at my door.
Who should I blame for my problems?
When I know that I am the core.

It's easy to blame the devil.
He's the root cause, haven't you heard?
Reject satan, you will upset satan
When you are learning of Christ and His word.

Remember that God knows your mission
He has given you untapped potential
As you prosper in life with new vision
Knowing God is very essential.

You see, God wants to strengthen your faith
Without trouble, you won't recognize Him.
There are times when you need to call Jesus.
He'll show up, then you will realize Him.

Don't continue to credit the enemy.
Know our savior and you'll persevere.
Lift your hands while you give him the glory.
Trust the Father, He will always be near.

The Funeral – It's The Remix

Today I've come to lay to rest the brokenness of me!
A force that stopped my growth, now I'm going to set me free.
In the casket, there before me lay my past, issues & pain.
The sunrise, my acceptance of my life's unhealthy gains.
The sunset, my decision to live kingdom & repent.
God has shown me who I am, not what I've been or where I went
Being victimized, afraid, left alone or in the dark
Bearing generational curses, with rejection from the start
Addictions, not nutritional, some medicinal, some relational,
Growing up, my dad was missing & that grief was devastational.
Taking detours of the low roads, not on Kingdoms' GPS.
With this casket in plain view, my past life's dead, it was a mess!
I was mourning loss of life, the blame and shame, it had to go.
With the weight of past pains heavy, 'I' was killing me, I know.
Drowning heavy, tearfully broken, grieving lifestyle had me shaking.
Holding on too much self-doubt, I thought God colored me forsaken.
Reminiscing of past hurts, all the nightmares were distracting.
It was time to kill the demons, kingdom lifestyle's more attractive
So, I questioned, is this death of me considered suicide?
The word says die to self, so that the NEW self can survive!
I killed the hurt, I killed the pain, Farewell! And now 'I' rise!

Life is over for that old me, no more lies and no more cries!

My decision – Bury my issues & heal from hurt, so 'I' can begin.

Releasing demons, breaking chains, a change of mindset so 'I' will win!

Just like the woman with issue of blood, enough was enough, give me His Hem

Killed my brokenness, said goodbye, and now Christ Jesus, here I am!

I am much more than my past! Fearfully & wonderfully made.

I am much more than a conqueror. In His WORD is where I've stayed.

So finally, I'm free, laying painful sorrows to rest.

Not missing what is gone, my new life, it suits me best

There's a home for this old brokenness, the last place I'll grieve you.

Now proceeding to the graveyard, where I will be leaving you

I am gifted, dead weights lifted, faith & mission greatly shifted

Its God I see and hearing clearly, I am no longer restricted

Finding JOY in my self-worth, I didn't know that 'I' existed

Now my kingdom lifestyle matters, I no longer will resist Him.

To Brokenness – Rest in Peace –
(Sunset -Life's Issues) – (Sunrise – God's Redemption)

W.O.M.E.N.

Wealthy warriors who are wise and washed of worldly sins.
Overcomers of oppression; opposition made to win.
Masters of our game; meeting men that we contest
Experiencing life's pain but expecting life at best
Nubians and new beings, numerous needs, never defined.
~~
We are women, yes, indeed who let Jesus change our minds.
Out of scriptures come the word, His foundation we must gain.
Making him priority so our lives will not be shamed.
Every woman is a queen, but she has to let it show.
Now un-covered in her being to reveal a Jesus glow.

M.O.T.H.E.R.

Magnificent mother and molder of me.
Observer of old and new trials to be.
Triumphantly teaching of right and wrong.
Heroically, singing inherited songs.
Exceptionally eager with favor and grace.
Righteous believer who has won her race.
~~
Motivator, My dear, and mother of me.
Obedient! She loves unconditionally.
Trusting and hearing her child's request.
Healing by prayer helps her love me the best.
Extending her hand as she smiles with pride.
Rewards to our mother. Her child by her side.

You All Holy Now, Right?

Yo' cuz! Where you been? we've been trying to reach ya
I hear you've been spending some time with the
preacher
We wanted to hang out and party tonight
Oh, that's right, we forgot, **you all holy now, right?**

Come on now, cuz, you got us all laughing!
We remember you used to love men with a passion
You used to drink more than the fish in the sea
You knew every drug from the A to the Z

So now you're so saved, you seem like a foreigner
You act like you're dead, wait let's call the coroner
This can't be you, Cuz, and you loved to dance
Got a man out there for ya, might be your last chance

OK, Cuz, you asked me, now I'm gonna tell you
I thought long and hard about heaven or hell, yo!
I remember my past which I tried to forget
For I know that I haven't thanked God enough yet

For bringing me through, in hard times, when I cried
When I almost got killed or when I could have died
Go on to your party and tear up the floor
'Cause when it's all over you'll be looking for more

God is now my main man, I don't need the last chance
I have joy, I have GOD, and I still have my dance
I now praise him daily, I sleep well at night
I live for the WORD, as His word is what's right

Now you're looking around, but you're curious, doubter!
You're jealous, my life has been better without ya!
I finally found Jesus, I don't need your crowd
I don't think you heard me, I'm saved and I'm proud'

*Cuz! You're not saved yet but don't stop till you've
tried it.
When you welcome His love, you'll be healed, no denying
it
My glow speaks for me, so I don't have to rave
So, I strive to be Holy, I'm so glad I'm saved*

Glory be to God the Almighty!

Your Love Sucks

So, when we decided, we were going to have a
relationship,
I thought that it was my thought,
but it was already your plan, scheming man!
I thought you had a 'right' love, I was excited for love

Finally!

You told me that 'I loved you already'
Why so? Probably because of my actions,
Me, saying too much, giving too much, and doing too
much, way too soon

So! Your role was to play standoffish, while closing in
for the kill
'Oh, don't talk about love, just have a good time!', you
said.
You wanted your party life, while having a 'stand in'
make-believe wife

Me, being naïve, I stepped right in and fit the bill
I had not yet swallowed the living single pill
Your camouflage was perfect, hiding in front of enemy
lines
You appeared as someone heaven sent
All the while you were like Eve's serpent, offering fruit
from a forbidden tree
God had already said 'Don't!' but once again, I ignored
his words
Well, by my own hand I gained a man

Full of stress, drama, and strain, leading to a different
kind of pain
The benefits not a return on my investment
Shiny and sharp, dressed to impress

Smile like a Cheshire cat, cologne from the best
You're tough demeanor all part of the game
Me, lonely and desperate, I have me to blame
I was optimistic, but you were narcissistic
Wanting to shine and be a celebrity, a star

That's who you were from whence you came, from afar
So military, meticulous, on the surface an imposter
As I came closer on the surface, I recognized the monster
Your lies, very promising, but you had to have your way
Such a star, celebrity, as I sat there, on display
Mr. Manure, wine connoisseur, Mr. GQ, photo jazz, man!
You were a magnet, drawing attention was your plan
They knew you were with me, but you told them 'It's okay!'

God reminded me that I was blindsided by my own hand
Instead of waiting for the right man
You thought it was all good, I did not know you'd be a schmuck!
But I must tell you, I learned the real you,
We failed in love because, **YOUR LOVE SUCKS!**

Chapter 4
A Tree of Righteousness

A Tree Of Righteousness- Intro

Tree – *Basic Definition* – A tree is a plant that has grown from a seed planted, with a wood foundation (trunk), with roots that extend into the ground. It usually grows tall and branches that grow outward. Leaves or fruit will grow from the branches. There are many types of trees in many heights, forms, and size.

Tree is also defined as a base for something to grow out, such as a family tree, where the tree begins with the previous ancestors and shows how each family member branched out by having their own children and it shows relation and generations.

The Lifetime of a Tree - A tree can live for ages, longer than you or I.

Trees may suffer severe damage, such as thunderstorms or hurricanes, but they have also survived storms, droughts, fires, and remain standing.

My nickname is *Tree*, I was initially given that name by an usher, Lucy B. Williams, in the year 2000, and it has grown with me since. In the worldly roads I have traveled, that name followed me, in the event world, on the dance floor and in previous relationship, I was Tree. It has since become part of my social media and pen name (Tree Pears).

I have been that Tree that has started out, growing from a seed, the seed planted from my mother, Ludie M. Pearsall, and my father, Albert James Miller. With some of the things I've lived through, hurt, pain, rejection, low self-esteem, I would wonder why I was born, and what was my purpose here. Now I understand. It was God's plan for that seed to be planted. He has a plan and potential for every seed planted. For Him, the way you **become** is not as important as the fact that you **became**.

My growth into the Tree I have become today, has been strengthened by the branches I have produced, my daughter and grandchildren, my families and relationships, my knowledge I have acquired in the healthcare field, and the knowledge I have acquired in accepting Christ and continually learning of Him and the doctrine of the kingdom. God's assignment for me was to share my testimony, telling a story that gives God the glory. If you didn't know, now you know.

Becoming a Tree of Righteousness was always my destiny even before I knew it. God had a plan. He shaped and molded me, had me weather some storms, go through some droughts and fires. There were times when I really got burnt, touch not the unclean thing. Through it all I am still standing, like that old, weathered Tree. I eat of His good fruit daily, so that He can produce good fruit within me. Each day, I become more of that Righteous Tree than I was before because. You must remain teachable; in Him you can never know it all. You cannot master the master in the kingdom. I desire Him daily!

I am thanking you all in advance for allowing me to take you on a poetic journey with my poems, stories and stoetries. I've had more to say than what I realized. What you do for Christ will last. My heart is for Him; therefore, it is for you all. Remember, I am just one Tree in the forest of many. Much Love to all of you, **Tree Pears**.

Living the Kingdom – Scripture References

Matthew 6:33

But **seek ye first** the kingdom of God, and his righteousness; and all these things shall be added unto you.

Plain and simple – seek first the Kingdom of God, no other!

Luke 12:32-40 NIV

[2] "Do not be afraid, little flock, for your Father has been pleased to give you the kingdom.

The Kingdom is a gift the Father wants to give us, but you must be born again.

Matthew 4 v17

[17] From that time on Jesus began to preach, "Repent, for the kingdom of heaven has come near."

Repent does not just mean to say you are sorry for the past sins, but to also change your mindset so that going forward you will live right, within the kingdom, for Christ.

John 3:3 [3] Jesus replied, "Very truly I tell you, no one can see the kingdom of God unless they are born again.

If you are not born again, you will not receive the kingdom.

Mark 1 14 After John was put in prison, Jesus went into Galilee, proclaiming the good news of God. [15] "The time has come," he said. "The kingdom of God has come near. Repent and believe the good news!"

We must continue to share His good news, so that lives will change, mindsets will change, and we will receive the kingdom by becoming born again and becoming a tree of righteousness.

Matthew 5

¹Now when Jesus saw the crowds, he went up on a mountainside and sat down. His disciples came to him, ² and he began to teach them.

The Beatitudes - God said:

³Blessed are the poor in spirit, for theirs is the kingdom of heaven.
⁴ Blessed are those who mourn, for they will be comforted.
⁵ Blessed are the meek, for they will inherit the earth.
⁶ Blessed are those who hunger and thirst for righteousness, for they will be filled.
⁷ Blessed are the merciful, for they will be shown mercy.
⁸ Blessed are the pure in heart, for they will see God.
⁹ Blessed are the peacemakers, for they will be called children of God.
¹⁰ Blessed are those who are persecuted because of righteousness,
    for theirs is the kingdom of heaven.

Jesus taught that the kingdom of heaven belongs to those who are hungry for His righteousness, and desire the kingdom, but must become born again to receive it.

Colossians 13-14 "For he has rescued us from the dominion of darkness and brought us into the kingdom of the Son he loves, in whom we have redemption, the forgiveness of sins."

Rescued, brought into. Redeemed, and forgiven. With the kingdom, we receive all of the above.

Matthew 13:44

"The **kingdom** of heaven is like treasure **hidden** in a field. When a man found it, he hid it again, and then in his joy went and sold all he had and bought that field."

The kingdom in the bible is 'hidden in plain view', we have read the scriptures many times, but are now just getting the correct understanding. Don't stop reading, don't stop studying. Study to show thyself approved and understand there is more to becoming a 'Tree of Righteousness' than salvation. God sent Jesus to die for our sins and give the gift of salvation, so that we will not live in eternal hell because of sin. However, until we transition to eternal life in the kingdom, we can experience the kingdom life here on earth, continuing to bear His fruits.

"Above all, love each other deeply, because love covers over a multitude of sins." **1 Peter 4:8**

Looking

Looking *for love in all the wrong places*
For all the wrong reasons, in all the wrong spaces
Receiving from birth the love from my mother
Her love so very different, but yet was like no other

Looking *for love, from my cool and loving father,*
In childhood I discovered, his love was shared with others
I loved all my sisters and my brothers too,
But Daddy was gone, so my heart remained blue

I looked *for acceptance amongst many peers*
Reputation now smeared & rejection turned to tears
Looking for love like I saw the world embrace
Always wanted a love that anyone could trace

A lover *that cared and kept a smile on my face*
A lover who gifted with jewelry and lace
Looking *for love that would not break my heart*
But my search was not smart, often, hurt played a part

Looking *for freedom, didn't know enough then*
Protected by Mother, her love was tough then
I moved from her space 'cause I wanted much more
Then I finally understood what she prayed daily for

Couldn't *wait on God, needed love my way*
It was not agape, but more selfish, risqué
If you are soul searching, tell me what do you see?
In my soul now I'm free, bearing fruits plain to see
Still Looking for love, *but I'm seeking Him first*
After numerous hurts, Christ's Love quenched my thirst

Now I know of real love and the kingdom at hand
Finally found love that's true, only 'seeking' one man

Righteous Scripture References

There are at least 291 scriptures I the bible regarding righteousness. I have chosen a few that are my favorites to list here for you. I suggest you review when you can to understand what is important about God's righteousness, walking upright and becoming a tree of righteousness. Righteousness is a characteristic of the Trinity (The Father, the Son & The Holy Spirit). God expects you to become righteous so that you can share in this gift with Him, but you must be born again. Verses are from the KJV translation.

Isaiah 61:3 (KJV)

To appoint unto them that mourn in Zion, to give unto them beauty for ashes, the oil of joy for mourning, the garment of praise for the spirit of heaviness; that they might be called *trees of righteousness*, the planting of the Lord, that he might be glorified.

To become righteous is to have the Lord planted in you, receiving His good fruit, characteristics of strength, integrity, joy and living by God's commandments, like a seed that is nurtured and fed and flourishes into a strong Tree that bears His fruit.

Genesis 15:6

And he believed in the Lord; and he counted it to him for **righteousness**.

Believing is the first part of receiving His holy word and becoming righteous.

Deuteronomy 6:25

And it shall be our **righteousness**, if we observe to do all these commandments before the Lord our God, as he hath commanded us.

An act of obeying the commandments of God is an act of righteousness.

1 Samuel 26:23

The Lᴏʀᴅ render to every man his **righteousness** and his faithfulness; for the Lᴏʀᴅ delivered thee into my hand today, but I would not stretch forth mine hand against the Lᴏʀᴅ's anointed.

The Lord wants us to be just as righteous and faithful as He is, the Lord will extend these fruits to us, we should not act against His anointing

2 Samuel 22:21

The Lᴏʀᴅ rewarded me according to my **righteousness**: according to the cleanness of my hands hath he recompensed me.

The Lord saw righteous fruit in me, and He has rewarded me.

Job 27:6

My **righteousness** I hold fast and will not let it go: my heart shall not reproach me so long as I live.

I will hold on to my righteousness.

Job 29:14

I put on **righteousness**, and it clothed me: my judgment was as a robe and a diadem.

Wear your righteousness, like the armor of God.

Psalm 7:17

I will praise the Lᴏʀᴅ according to his **righteousness**: and will sing praise to the name of the Lᴏʀᴅ most high.

I will praise His name at all times, in righteousness and truth.

Psalm 31:1

In thee, O Lᴏʀᴅ, do I put my trust; let me never be ashamed: deliver me in thy **righteousness**.

Lord, I trust in you, deliver me from thy shame, I am ready for a righteous change. Because of you I cannot remain the same.

Proverbs 11:30

The fruit of the **righteous** is a tree of **life**, and the one who is wise saves lives.

*Lord, thank you for allowing me to be a Tree in this life, and to be wise enough to learn of you, your kingdom doctrine, and share the fruit you have given me; that saved and changed my life. This fruit, from the **tree of righteousness**, is not strange fruit, but is the fruit that we are fed and the fruit that we should eat. Selah!*

Stuck in a Place Called God

I am stuck in a place called God, even though the stormy roads I've trod
I have thought this out thoroughly and have come to understand
It is not that I cannot command, be demanding or
Play the tune of a different band. It is because of God's hand

That I focus on my vision and carry out my mission
It was always God's decision that I not move in another direction
Becoming bound to His divine connection
'Cause I am stuck in a place called God

I am stuck in a place called God, even though the stormy roads I've trod.
I was at the crossroads with a sign of directions,
Each sign pointing differently, being confused by a few
But the question for me was, 'Which way do I go?', 'Is God there, too?'
If not, do not push me, I shall not be moved.
If 'there' is where God is, then I will go! If not then
Hell, no!
'Cause He laid His life down, it's a NEW life I've found, His word has me bound
I am stuck in a place called God.
I am stuck in a place called God, even though the stormy roads I've trod.
I am trapped like the hunter that leaves the snare for the wild beasts or bear.
God is the hunter in the wilderness. He catches you best when you're under duress.
I am His captive, caught by Christ's snare. I cannot be freed, even if I dared.

People look, some will talk. They may not agree. Keep

looking, His fruit you will see in me.
Although often reminded of what I have lost, the views
are distorted, and some eyes are crossed.
I have found peace sharing His ministry, knowing that
Jesus has rescued me
As I am stuck in a place called God.

**I am stuck in a place called God, even though the
stormy roads I've trod.**
Captured, by the enemy, but God had the remedy
His goal for me was ministry. He saved my life, just in
time.
He's coming for you! So, stand in line
From salvation's beginning, Jesus lightened the load, He
padded my blow,

Even then, life became tougher. Training in the trenches
was much rougher, with longsuffering.
He never stuttered or muttered, but I uttered because
of His gaze finding out, perseverance pays!
As I worship and give Him praise, I am promoting my
vision these days.
Yes! I am stuck in a place called God.
**I am stuck in a place called God, even though the
stormy roads I've trod.**
Being constantly reminded of what I've lost, as a
Christian, I am constantly paying the cost.
There have been roadblocks on the paths I've crossed,
Unless I tell, you will not see my loss.
I have put on the mask, but now, I take it off.
I've gained much favor from the Father and Son, many
battles have been won.
God will create testimonies for you!
The glory is His after you come through.
You will be stuck in a place called God.
**I am stuck in a place called God, even though the
stormy roads I've trod.**
My new fragrance is a Jesus scent. It is called **'Priceless**

Commitment'.
Trapped by God! *The rewards are greater, so expect the haters.*
You ask. Can I still trust him If I do not see him? Oh yes! It's because I believe Him.
How do you think I am still standing? As my right-hand, he stands beside me.
I have even learned to love my enemy. Better yet, I've learned how to love me, better!
But how will I survive? You see, my God is alive.
I am revived! And still, I thrive. Trapped by God, I strive.
As I am stuck in a place called God.

You see, I am stuck in a place called God, even though the stormy roads I've trod.
From the East, West, North and South.
Can you understand the words coming out of my mouth?
Caught in His trap, I cannot look back, although there is a constant attack.
I'll run the race on God's track.
When I look at my goals, accomplishments, and events,
From receiving my God, I haven't been the same since.
As I am stuck in a place called God.

I am stuck in a place called God even though the stormy roads I've trod.
The same way some folks use too much salt,
I cannot do anything without picking God up and putting God on it. Repeatedly, I've expressed.
If God isn't in it, then don't begin it. Call me a fool, but I would only be a fool without God.
I am a fool *in love with God, and He loves fools and babies*
God has trapped me! Jesus, hold on to me.
I am not trying to be free of thee,
As I am stuck in a place called God!

A Seed Planted

God found me at my lowest place
I didn't know to seek His face
He called my name, took hurt away
Didn't understand what He was trying to say

I am the seed planted, my soul now a tree
His fruit I now bear, from the branches of me
Others helped by the leaves of my testimony
Becoming His child has strengthened me

'Lord, love me, help me, change me, break me
Hold me, mold me, bless me, shape me
Pick me up from off the ground,
Teach me how to know you'

'Wrap me in your loving arms
Comfort me when all are gone
Rescue me with your caress,
Teach me how to know you'

I lost my mind then I found You!
His righteous seed, and mercies, new
I've Become a Tree standing! Weathering storms
Branches extended, Glory keeping me warm

My roots, foundation, becoming strengthened
The fruit I am bearing, now ripe for the mention
The one I'm becoming, the kingdom represents
A rooted Tree of righteousness

'Lord, love me, help me, change me, break me
Hold me, mold me, bless me, shape me
Pick me up from off the ground,
Teach me how to know you'

'Wrap me in your loving arms
Comfort me when all are gone
Rescue me with your caress,
Teach me how to know you.

God's plan for me was to become a Tree of Righteousness.

This picture includes my beautiful daughter, Syreeta, at 2 years old.

www.ingramcontent.com/pod-product-compliance
Lightning Source LLC
Chambersburg PA
CBHW071407120626
46546CB00002B/848